Hoshinjutsu

The Art of Esoteric Budo

法心武道

By Rob Williams, Soke of Hoshinbudoryu

Published by Hoshin Budo Ryu

Hoshinbudoryu
www.Hoshin.us

Written by Rob Williams
Formatting and cover design by Jared Guinn

ISBN 978-0-578-03575-8

"Rob Williams has a massage system developed just for us that is awesome. Our Chi Kung system is head and shoulders above everyone else and our yoga is going to be awesome too."

Glenn J Morris, soke

Hoshinjutsu *The Art of Esoteric Budo*

Table of Contents

Preface

This book on Hoshinjutsu is intended for anyone, in or out of martial arts, seeking to improve and balance their skills at conquering life's problems, roadblocks and demons. In this book, Rob-soke describes his journey, experiences and observations of a variety of teachers and philosophies, which all contribute to his life path currently found as soke of the Hoshinbudoryu.

Soke Williams was both a great student and great friend of the late "Doc" Glenn Morris. Several years ago, in a personal discussion with Doc he confided in me that Rob Williams would be the one to take over as soke upon his passing. Unfortunately, this event occurred much too soon for anyone. However, Rob-soke has consistently displayed the passion, compassion and wisdom of a truly great leader.

Soke Rob Williams is one of the few naturally gifted all-round martial artists. The first time I saw him move I was amazed at the grace and clarity of his movement. He was able to move precisely where the chi energy of the circumstances deemed necessary. During a break at a training session one time Rob demonstrated a forward roll, while holding a drink in his hand and not spilling a drop.

This book describes the history and heritage of Hoshin, including the key leaders, students and influences that have made Hoshin the legendary ryu of our time. Hoshinjutsu is an excellent companion book to *Path Notes of an American Ninja Master*, by Dr. Glenn Morris.

Dr. John Porter

Introduction

This book is dedicated to all who are interested in the Hoshin path of personal development. I would like to thank all of my students and friends who encouraged me to share my experiences. I would like to thank all of the Hoshinbudoryu Shihan and Sensei for helping carry on the teachings of Dr. Morris and the Hoshinjutsu system. Special thanks to Guru Santiago Dobles for sharing traditional Silat and being pivotal in organizing the KAP (Kundalini Awakening Process) program. Thanks to Tao Semko for his help with CD, DVD and web production and his sharing of Tantra. Thanks to Dr. John Porter aka Fudosan for the research he and Dr. Morris began nearly 30 years ago. Thanks to Tom Zeblisky for making wonderful training weapon for Doc's ryu and now mine. Big thanks go to Doug and Michelle Tweedy for keeping us current in the teachings of the Bujinkan. Huge thanks to Jared Guinn for formatting the ryu manuals, books and anything else I need. Most of all thanks to my wife Lenna, who shares my love for Hoshin and helps me with running our ryu and keeping the members organized. Loving thanks to my daughter Trinity Rain whose curiosity is a constant reminder of the awe and wonder of new discoveries. And of course, eternal thanks go out to our mentor Dr. Glenn J. Morris for sharing his life and inspiring us to go beyond the physical.

This book is my perspective on the subjects of Hoshinjutsu, Chi Kung, Kundalini and esotericism. This is my attempt at explaining esoteric training based on the experiences of my friends, colleagues and students. The information presented comes from conversations with Hoshin Shihan who actively run training groups, friends of Glenn's that were there when Hoshin began, my personal experiences and my training under Dr. Morris.

None of this stuff is hard edged, though we have a serious amount of research and empirical testing which shows us the methods are working. Much of the 'spiritual' phenomenon that we have experienced have cross cultural descriptions that for the most part seem to be the basis for many ancient and modern belief systems. Energies, spirits, archetypes or whatever else you want to call them have been described by practically every culture. This book is my opinion. Take it or leave it. I followed Glenn's methods and they worked. Most who read this book have probably read Doc's books. I have omitted some names that seemed irrelevant or would cause undue scrutiny of people I have trained or dealt with personally. This book is about my involvement with Dr. Glenn Morris and Hoshin. It is my hope that this book will help people understand the Hoshinjutsu system and philosophy, and maybe provide an explanation for something they have already experienced. In reality, no one has all the answers or can tell us what to believe. Whether you accept my interpretation or not is up to you. Try out the exercises and have fun.

Rank in martial arts was never important to me. After being whooped pretty good as a young boy by the neighborhood bully, I had a strong desire to learn to protect myself. I grew up training in various martial arts such as Karate, Tae Kwon Do, Shaolin Five Fist Kung-fu (the old system where slow powerful movements are used for each animal) and other hard style martial arts. I always felt that the more I knew the safer I would be. As a young man I trained in hard Chi Kung, Iron Palm and Dim Mak bird pecking exercises for the purpose of developing my body's weapons. I wanted to toughen my hands and knuckles so that I wouldn't get injured in a fight. Breaking bricks and boards were not my goal. It was apparent that physics and motion are the keys to breaking stuff.

Ninjutsu was introduced to me at a young age during the ninja boom of the 80's. After reading Stephen Hayes' books, like many, I was intrigued. Back then, Stephen Hayes was the main person trying to explain Ninpo. He used a western way of explaining the Japanese concept of the Godai (5 elemental manifestations). This interpretation of the art changed over the years as more and more people became instructors of Bujinkan and would travel to Japan to train with Hatsumi-soke.

While living in Maryland as a teenager, I was lucky enough to have a Bujinkan Ninjutsu practitioner in the neighborhood. I had noticed him walking into the woods with a bo staff and decided I would ask him what he was up to. Up to that point I just knew of him as T-bone; a neighbor we would ride dirt bikes in the woods with. I was introduced to the training being conducted during the early years of Ninjutsu in the US. We played with the Kihon Happo (8 basics), San Shin no Kata (3 hearts exercises), Gotonpo (5 element concealment), sword, chains, shuriken, shuko (hand claws) and an array of traditional weapons. It was so much fun playing ninja.

I began studying Jow Ga Kempo, which is a technical Chinese street fighting system based on tiger style kung-fu. I eventually became an assistant instructor for the dojo and was even invited to go to China to train and compete. My Sifu was very strict. He didn't like us training in other martial arts. I was sparring with a class mate to prepare for our National competition to be held in Washington D.C. He was getting pretty nasty and throwing blows that wouldn't be legal in the competition. He punched at my face and I slid back into Ichimonji to avoid the shot to my head, rocked forward over my lead knee and palm struck him in the chest, sending him flying. I didn't see our instructor watching. I was not using Jow Ga. My Sifu yelled for us to stop. He asked me to come to his office. "What else have you been studying?" "Uhhh, I have been playing around with a friend of mine." I explained nervously.

That was it. I was told that I couldn't train in his dojo anymore. I was upset yet more frustrated at the narrow minded approach he had to training. I liked the freedom of movement and adaptability of Ninpo. I have never trained with a Bujinkan practitioner who told me that his way was the only way. I am a strong believer in searching far and wide to get as much knowledge as possible. I like to go with the flow. I usually stayed with a teacher until I had learned what I could or they got too arrogant. Shortly after my fall out with the Sifu, I moved to Virginia.

In the fall of 1993, I was sitting in my room playing guitar when a feeling came over me that I needed to visit the book store. I walked into Walden Books in the local mall, went to the martial arts section and saw *Path Notes* on the shelf. I read the back cover and flipped through the chapters which mentioned things I had been noticing. Seemed like a great read. Around the same time I found another Bujinkan practitioner. I was teaching him and his son guitar lessons and happened to have *Path Notes* under my chair. He looked at the book and asked if he could hold it. He pointed the cover at his son and asked if it looked familiar. The cover has Glenn's Bujinkan Godan certificate kanji. His son replied to me that his dad had the same certificate. Steve Polly had trained under Dick Severance in Florida. Polly and I played one on one for a few years. Once in a while I would bring a friend to beat on so he could coach me. We worked primarily from the Ten Chi Jin no Maki (Book of heaven, earth and man) which is a much more organized curriculum than the loose knit training I had been exposed to earlier. Polly remembered Doc from the old training groups. Like many Bujinkan practitioners, he had no interest in chi or energy phenomenon. He would laugh when I would bring up the Godai and tell me I was going off the deep end again. Having a 7th Dan in Shorin Ryu Shorinkan Karate, he is a very practical fighter. I would teach a few friends what I could and ran a small Ninpo training group.

After contacting Glenn through email I decided I wanted to study Hoshin in depth. I had been practicing the exercises in *Path Notes* and they were working. I began distance training in Hoshin under Doc and started adding Hoshin to my training group. After my first visit to meet him, I was convinced that his system was what I had been looking for. I incorporated Hoshinjutsu into my Ninpo training. We talked about Ninpo and he found it funny that I shared his perspective. I had played with old school Bujinkan folks who stressed sensitivity drills and kihon happo using the Godai thought forms and dynamic. Once I tested for Shodan in Hoshin Jutaijutsu, my training group became a Hoshin class. Doc also became my primary Bujinkan Shidoshi, sharing his perspective on Ninpo Taijutsu and the ura (hidden) training he learned from Hatsumi. I am one of the few people he personally promoted in Bujinkan Budo Taijutsu.

Shidoshi Doug Tweedy of the Bujinkan Shima Dojo in Richmond, Virginia is my source for the current Bujinkan training. He is also a Sandan in Hoshinbudoryu Jutaijutsu. He trains under Shihan Ed Martin, other Shihan in the US and travels to Japan to train with the Japanese Shihan and Hatsumi. Like Doc, Ninpo is one of my hobbies. My expertise is in Hoshin Jutaijutsu, which is a different system than Ninpo.

Having played with many styles of martial arts for nearly 30 years, and taught Hoshin for well over a decade, I have seen and done many things that are beyond normal explanation. Dr. Glenn Morris' viewpoint was fascinating to me in that normally hidden information was offered openly. *Path Notes of an American Ninja Master* by Dr. Morris reveals many secrets of internal development that are usually kept for senior practitioners of traditional martial and spiritual systems. Much of what I read in that book made sense, as I had already noticed energy phenomenon while practicing internal and physical martial arts. It was nice to read a master's book that verified what I had experienced. After you learn the way energy feels, looks and works, you will realize that it's not as otherworldly as is commonly thought. Doc always took a scientific viewpoint to esoteric training. Bio-energetic systems in our bodies are electrical. Chi works similarly to magnetism. Developing chi and working with it can be learned by anyone. Hoshin, in my opinion, offers the most efficient way of accomplishing it. Hoshin is the map. You must make the journey.

Chapter 1

Hoshin History

Hoshin Jutaijutsu is a complete system of physical, mental and spiritual development. This art, which was created by Dr. Glenn J. Morris in the early 80's, was originally designed in a college atmosphere and was a collection of nasty strategies Doc had learned through fights, the army and playing with martial arts. Dr. Morris had trained in many traditional martial arts. He was also fond of the Quick Kill system taught to US servicemen.

Prior to the 1980's, the majority of martial arts schools in the US taught primarily Karate or Judo. As more and more martial arts were introduced to American culture there was a movement to try to blend different styles either by offering a one school teaches all styles opportunity; or to try to combine what fits and works best for the founder of a new system. Kung-fu was rare, especially outside the west coast. Ninpo was just being introduced in America by Stephen K. Hayes. When Doc saw the footwork of Ninpo, and how it related to different emotions, he was instantly impressed.

Doc first attended a Ninpo seminar, taught by Stephen Hayes, in the early 1980's. It was an Earth seminar. Doc was in the early process of forming his own martial art system. He brought one of his first students, Toffesse, to the Ninpo seminar to help with analyzing new ideas and concepts for Hoshinjutsu. It was at this seminar Doc met John Porter. John Porter had been studying Ninpo for a few years so during the seminar he was able to explain a lot of the philosophy of Ninpo to Doc and Tof. Of most significance was the elemental theory of the Godai Kata. The Godai Kata is based on the theory of moving around in and balancing opposite emotions and actions. It is a psychological principle with documented use of over 3,000 years.

In developing his new system of martial arts, Doc was interested in taking the best from a variety of systems and then adding a concept that he had developed himself. What intrigued Doc most about Ninpo was the footwork. Rather than having footwork that was designed to do a technique, here was a concept of using footwork relative to one's current emotional state of mind. The theory is that the emotional state causes your body to move a certain way, and/or that by moving your body a certain way you change your emotional state. This emotional connection is the core of Hoshin training.

It was always important to Doc to include healing arts with the martial aspects. His compassionate philosophy was that if you were going to harm someone you would also need to heal them. But most importantly, Doc included the esoteric aspects of martial arts.

What is unique about Hoshin is that esoteric information and lessons are part of the 'everyday' class instruction. Most martial arts instructors will talk about the esoteric concepts 'in theory'. In fact, it is quite common for martial arts instructors to tell students that when they get to a level 'advanced enough' that they can start learning the esoteric skills associated with martial arts. It is important to note that whenever you hear a martial arts instructor make this kind of statement, it is probably code for "I don't really know anything about esoteric practices and hopefully you will find someone who does." To an extreme, there are a few martial arts instructors who will claim that esotericism does not exist. (This is an example of the limited and restrictive teachings of martial arts that have many students looking at Hoshin as a practical system.) In contrast, Doc taught esoteric concepts in every class that he was a part of, as teacher or student. Within the first few minutes of your first Hoshin class, you will be able to clearly know that this is a very unique and powerful system. Seeing and feeling energy and intention are the kihon or basic technique in Hoshinjutsu.

Doc's early animal familiar was the bear. He took to heart the Native American expression "If you're going to be a bear, you might as well be a grizzly." This pre-Hoshin grizzly bear attitude, which was essential Earth and Fire, was the core of the understanding of how Doc approached the physical techniques of martial arts. Conveniently, John Porter was adept at the Water and Wind aspects of physical techniques. This early friendship, which shared ideas and supported weakness, provided a strong basis to fully develop the concepts of Hoshin.

Doc's later animal familiar was the spider. He identified with many of the spiders attributes. Among the many attributes is the aggressive nature and fighting ability of the spider. If you put several rabbits in the same space you are going to end up with a lot of rabbits. If you put several spiders in one space you are going to end up with one spider. In this aspect, Doc was able to, at least neutralize, any opponent or opposition he faced. However, being that there is only one spider, indicates the loneliness that he experienced and identified with throughout his personal life. I believe that Doc changed from the bear to the spider over the years as his approach to martial arts combat changed. While developing and teaching the principles of Hoshin he learned the value of hiding, stealth and how to deliver a quick fatal strike with the least amount of overt effort. Even though both the bear and spider possess a lethal strike,

Doc learned to appreciate the subtleness and grace of the spider over the abrasive brute force of the grizzly.

Consciously or subconsciously, Hoshin was created for people that didn't fit into other martial arts styles. All of the initial students (and over 90% of the current students) had trained in other, more traditional martial arts styles. Collectively, they found other martial arts styles to be restrictive and limiting in the information taught. Some styles were primarily block-kick-punch, some were just about throws or grappling and some were just about stick fighting. At the time, none of the martial arts openly taught healing and esoteric skills. Doc attended some of the early American Ninja Festivals, before they were called Tai Kai. The early national ninja conferences were held at a camp ground near Middletown, OH. Participants stayed in bunk houses with as many as 20 participants to a house. These early ninja conferences serve as the format for today's Tai Kai and other multi-skill weekend seminars. Prior to the 1980's, this kind of training was non-existent in martial arts teachings in America. Doc wanted to implement this format in his system. Having weekly training classes, and then hosting a few large weekend seminars with multiple classes on different topics within the system.

During the time between his first annual Ninpo fest and his second, Doc developed the 'MAPS' inventory. Initially MAPS was an acronym for 'Martial Arts Personality Scale'. Later, when he used this tool with business leaders, it was known as the 'Management Attitude and Personality Scale'. The MAPS inventory was used as a guide for John Porter's doctorate dissertation on 'Three Dimensional Personality'; which in turn was used for the concepts in *Quantum Crawfish*. John Porter and Doc Morris shared and worked through many of the philosophical principles which have since been unified into the Hoshin system. Doc was not only a great teacher, but a great student. He took the time, effort and money to make several trips to Japan to train directly with 'the Boss.'

Doc's office at Hillsdale College was an interior corner

office on the second floor of the Dow Center Building. His office door window was covered with a decal of a katana sword. His first groups of students at Hillsdale College were composed primarily from Sigma Chi Fraternity and some defensive lineman from the Hillsdale College football team. Doc taught the lineman how to sense the energy and intent of the blocking offensive lineman, and then which element response would be the best counter move. The second year that Doc taught Hoshin to the football team members, Hillsdale College was NAIA National Champions.

The weekend Hoshin festivals or get-togethers were generally scheduled on Homecoming weekend in the fall and May Day weekend in the spring. This way there would be lots of strange people on campus, many of whom would look out of place or even accidentally go into an area or building that they should probably not be in. This made great cover to conduct clandestine activities. One common activity was to cause some confusion among the fraternities then sit on the roof of the Sigma Chi porch and watch the confusion unfold during the regular weekend activities. It was like watching a secret subplot to a live play.

Saturday evening was generally reserved to go to the Slayton Arboretum. Here, members of the seminar and a few selected guests would sit around the campfire, sharing stories and getting to know one another better. This was a traditional event until the weekend someone decided to bring a couple of buckets of fried chicken to the evening campfire. Unfortunately, although the meal was delicious, not all the bones were picked up and put in the trash. So the next morning, someone found a lot of chicken bones by the campfire and deducted that it was a result of an animal sacrifice. Indirectly that might be true, but not in the sense of ceremonial animal sacrifices. So, the conservative university administration put an end to the Hoshin class using the arboretum. Doc's tenure at Hillsdale was short lived after that. He continued to teach Hoshin through seminars and private instruction.

Hoshin continued to evolve as each instructor learned the core and applied it to what they already had. The karate people had a focus on hitting and kicking, the judoka would have a judo Hoshin, etc. Because of the emphasis on meditation and chi development, the internal exercises were added to what each person knew, and the system became scattered. As long as instructors taught Hoshin Tao Chi Kung and the basic techniques, Doc really didn't care what else was being shown. Also, at the time Ninpo was the system most commonly practiced by Hoshin students, so the core Hoshin techniques began to disappear as less than a handful of people had actually learned the complete system from Soke Morris.

In the mid 90's Doc filmed the Hoshin teacher training tapes. These were designed to get the teachers all on the same page. Doc made them available to the public to try and get Hoshin to people who couldn't come to seminars or lived too far to train with a Hoshin instructor. He demonstrated the basic techniques but mixed up some of the belt information as he lectured. So there was some Water Belt and Fire Belt in the Earth Belt tape, etc. Earth Belt was the bulk of the physical system at that time. Anyone who trained during this time remembers how intricate the Earth Belt was. This turned away many would be students, as it took way too long to get through.

In 2001 Doc asked me to organize the system into palpable sections. The original manuals gave reading assignments with *Path Notes* and *Secrets of Shamanism* by Jose Stevens being the main two books for the course. Other books were assigned at the appropriate belt levels. The idea was to work with the chakra attitudes in order to open each center with an appropriate activity. He wanted students to get back to learning the core Hoshin Jutaijutsu techniques. I taught using the old manuals he had given me and worked on dissecting and perfecting Jutaijutsu techniques as well as the use of chi for healing and combat. I divided each belt into 3 sections. This way, students would have smaller chunks of information to focus on. Glenn would send me lists of techniques to add and/or remove. These techniques were then arranged into the appropriate elemental kyu grade. His main goal was to get the excessive Ninpo out. Hoshin is not Ninpo, though it is a similar path to self protection and development. Glenn used to joke "Its Ninja Lite … less time, more filling."

One of the reasons Doc asked me to work on organizing Hoshin was because I had developed a network of personally trained students and instructors. I had more experience with training and promoting Hoshin students than any other Hoshin instructor under Soke Morris. There are very few who learned the system at an advanced level. Because Doc was a little worried about the survival of the system, he promoted graciously and even promoted some students based on their attempt at friendship rather than their skill level. He mostly showed the basics at seminars, which was his way of getting everyone on the same page. I had refined his methods and tested them out with many students. I worked on getting a pure Hoshin knowledge base for the students and standardized the manuals and curriculum for Doc. He would often send students to me and would joke that I would, "Turn'em to the dark side."

I always encourage my student to practice meditation and chi cultivation. I would teach all the exercises in *Path Notes* including the mirror play, trading faces, micro and macrocosmic orbits, etc. These exercises are simple ways to observe esoteric phenomenon that is occurring in and around one's self. A student always knows where they are in their development in Hoshin. The primary goal, of course, is to develop usable amounts of chi. This essential aspect is what makes Hoshinjutsu strategy effective. Otherwise, there is no integration. Just prearranged movements, that might or might not work. The latter sounds risky to me.

With Hoshin we do the most with the least. When something comes along that is found to be smarter that what we are doing, it is tested and incorporated into the system. The pace for evolution in Hoshin was always at Nidan; where a student must add an original concept or improve an existing technique.

As each Black Belt added new techniques, Hoshin would improve gradually. Someone was promoted to Nidan every couple of years so new techniques were coming in very slowly. We would beat the snot out of each other to see if we could easily defeat new techniques.

Doc also asked me to study Russian Systema and learn the dynamics of how their techniques are done. After a few years of playing with it, I went to visit Doc and showed him what I had learned. There is a Youtube video of Doc and me training in his dojo during this particular visit. Search for Hoshin Budo. Systema is continuing to be incorporated into the Hoshinjutsu system at the Black Belt levels.

This can be seen in Nathaniel Bryant and Justin Henry of the Seven Centers Dojo in Lake Charles, La. They were/are the chief instructors of Soke Morris' Hombu Dojo. They trained with him several times a week and spoke with him just before he passed. Nate and Justin play a major role in carrying on Glenn's vision for improving our training. They have trained extensively in Systema and play very hard. I love to watch them train.

Hoshinjutsu is alive and well. There are quality instructors in our ryu who understand Glenn's vision for complete integration and can convey these methods to others. The classes continue to be taught and students continue to advance through the belt system. I teach Hoshin class every week and have a special mini seminar on particular topics the first Sunday of each month. I list all of these special events for the year on the Hombu class schedule page of our website www.hoshin.us. The Doc Morris memorial seminar is held the 1st Sunday in April. Hoshinfest is our annual gathering which is usually held in October.

Santiago and I have been comparing the similarities to Hoshin Jutaijutsu and traditional Pencak Silat. The elemental dynamics are amazingly similar. Santiago and Tao have begun teaching KAP seminars through live web conferences. With technology continuing to make it easier to connect with the world, we are getting Glenn's latest research out to the world. Hoshinjutsu is a living art. The strategies allow for adaptation to any circumstance. I am very proud to be a part of this amazing journey we are taking. To me, soke is simply the keeper of the tradition. It has nothing to do with rank. I am always a student on the Hoshin path. I feel extremely grateful to be a part of such a wonderful group of people and am excited to see where the ryu will be in the future.

Chapter 2

Hoshin Jutaijutsu

Each level of Hoshin is associated with a particular chakra in esoteric physiology. Chakras relate to the endocrine system and affect our attitude and energy levels. They are also related to nerve nexii on the spinal column. If you think in a particular way as you learn the techniques it allows you to connect the attitude with the physical movement. These responses will then be internalized and will surface depending on your feelings in a given situation. Hoshin uses the Godai movement model (Earth, Water, Fire, Wind, Void) as a way to work with each chakra and develop one's self into a balanced human being. The Godai is more than just physical movements. It is a model for integrating your emotions with a physical response so that true mind/body harmony can be achieved. You must practice the appropriate attitude, breathing dynamic and movement in order to train your instincts to give the proper response. This is actual mind, body with spirit (intent) working together. If you assume the elemental attitude of each chakra, it is very easy to assimilate the techniques.

Each element has a corresponding geometric shape that maximizes the effectiveness of the movements. Each chakra is also the pivot point for the elemental techniques and has opposing dynamics in their movement. They include stability, mobility, intensity and receptiveness. For example, the center of balance in Earth techniques is from the tail bone to the feet. You use up and down movement with the legs and body to control yourself and the weight of the attacker. In a lower stance you will have increased stability and decreased mobility. As you move your center of gravity up to each chakra you in turn change this dynamic.

The Water center is just below the navel. The hips shift to the side and back. This is more mobile and receptive but a little less stable. Fire movement is forward or short narrow diagonal motions that are driven from the solar plexus. Fire movement is more mobile and intense than Water but less stable and receptive. Wind movement is very high and light on your feet. You have maximum mobility and minimal stability. As you move through a fight these dynamics are in constant flux. You may be surprised by an attack and back away (Water), then quickly move in and crush (Earth) or go straight through the opponent (Fire). The techniques are designed to move your body based on your emotions. This is the essence of Hoshin Jutaijutsu heiho (*Weapon heart magic body skills strategy*). Doc would train this way and not give it much thought. It was just how he moved. He did what seemed appropriate at any given distance, and then applied pain in his usual unassuming way. Those who were lucky enough to watch Doc in action witnessed efficient fighting at its best.

Hoshin also follows a systematic approach to spiritual development. The system is designed to enhance ones physical and mental abilities by following exercises, meditations, physiological and psychological techniques that are specifically linked to a certain elemental dynamic. These activities open the chakra system and develop the inner faculties. We have been testing it for years with great success. It can be learned pretty quickly if you are training with an instructor who has integration and can transfer energy. All the Shihan instructors in Hoshinbudoryu are capable of chi transmission; I trained many of them. The rest are Doc's friends and personal students who developed chi on their own or under Doc's guidance.

Hoshin is not just a collection of techniques that work from other systems, with some meditation thrown in for good measure. Hoshin has a specific series of developmental strategies that allow for appropriate reactions to dangerous situations. At the higher levels, Hoshin Jutaijutsu doesn't look like martial arts per se. To observers, it appears that very little more than an accident occurred. It's a smart way to fight that allows one to conserve energy. In our system, there is no competition beyond personal goals. Students are there to help each other learn and practice dangerous situations in a controlled environment. Each belt is briefly outlined on the next pages.

White Belt

The White belt is earned in Hoshin. It shows your acceptance into the system, after demonstrating willingness to learn and progress. The strategy and philosophy of the Godai is explored. The elemental attitudes correspond to dynamics of movement and particular angles. Each element has an appropriate breathing technique that maximizes its effectiveness. This helps students understand the proper execution and timing of Godai movements.

Students learn the basic meditation technique for quieting and centering the mind. Doc used the "brain scrub" technique described in *Path Notes*. An easier way is to simply pay attention to your breathing. When you find your mind wandering, bring your attention back to the physical act of breathing. This is a one point focus. With practice, you'll be able to sit calmly for extended periods. Start with 10-15 minutes in the morning and evening. You're calming yourself down so that your mind becomes open to learning.

Hoshin Taiso (stretching and limbering exercises) and falling techniques are learned with attention to dispersing the energy of the fall. The key to Hoshin Jutaijutsu is soft, flexible knees and ankles. The arm and wrist stretches keep you limber, so your risk of injury from wrist lock techniques is minimized. Here is the basic idea. This will stretch you from head to toe. They can be added to any routine you currently practice. I used this sequence after my knee was fractured. My leg rehabilitated in half the time expected. Align your breathing with the movements. Exhale into the stretches and inhale as you return to the starting position. If done slowly, this sequence can become a moving meditation.

Hoshin Taiso

- Keeping your teeth touching, make small, then large circles with the head and neck. Imagine you are starting at the top of the neck and working down.
- Let your head hang down and grab the back of your head with the opposite side arm and pull down to stretch (Your right hand would cover the back left of your skull.)
- Shake your head while hanging down, vigorously from side to side.
- Pull fingers straight out, push them backward to stretch them.
- Pull on wrists, stretch in every direction. Hands palm to palm, pushing fingers back to stretch wrists.
- Push on wrists hanging down in a goose neck.
- Little birds (Loose circular swirls) to draw chi up to your hands
- Put an outside wrist lock on yourself. Touch your pinky's finger tip to your nose. Pull your hand down to your navel, or as far as you can while keeping your pinky touching the center line of your body.
- Spider stretches (Arms out to the sides, palms facing forward, stretching out and back at different heights. Imagine imitating the arms of a spider.

- Shepard stretch (Stretch arms 1 up, 1 down) Reach back as far as you can. Try to lock your hands behind your back. (Frees chi stuck between scapulas)
- Toe touches, back and legs straight, finger tips first then palms to the ground. Keep looking out in front of you, not down.
- Pull your knees to your chest while standing.
- Roll out on your ankles to prevent sprains.
- Go up on your toes. Spin your hips around, rotating your pelvis and knees. This works the lower back and hips.
- Spread your legs wide, feet facing outward. Shift your weight from one side to the other. If you know Ichimonji, you are just doing it from one leg to the other leg without stepping. This will stretch your hamstrings.
- Go into the splits. Let gravity ease you down. Once you are as far down as you can go, sit back while keeping your split. Exhale while trying to put your chest to the ground.
- Seiza stretch (Kneeling on legs) Put your thumbs in the middle of the soles of your feet. Let your head hang back as you push your pelvis upward into a body bridge.
- Caterpillar stretch. You are sitting up with your legs out straight and together. Exhale while trying to put your head to your knees. As you run out of air, inhale while sitting back up. Exhale while laying back, flat on the ground. Lift legs up and support your back as you try to put your knees near your ears.
- Lay down face up and perform deep belly breathing. On each exhale, as you relax all the muscles in your body, imagine you are melting into the floor. Scan your whole body for tension. Release it as you melt away.

Greetings to the Sun

Hoshin Sun Salutation is our way of working every muscle group with one simple exercise. The soft version of it can be seen in Yoga. We do it the Martial way:

15

Stand upright and reach for the sky as you go up on your toes, inhaling. As you exhale, drop your hands palm down and plant them in front of your feet. Jump back with both legs so that your arms are straight up like a push-up. Dip your pelvis to the floor as your head hangs back. This stretches the spine and sacrum. Jump your right foot out in front of your right hand as far as it will reach. Jump it back. Repeat with the left leg. After jumping back with the left leg, dip your waist to the floor again. Jump back up to your hands and stand up. Repeat. You can go up on your tippy toes as you reach up to work the calves and soleus muscle that supports them. There are variations to the hand positions. We use the palms, then the fists, finger tips and back of the wrists. If can do 12 a day (3 sets of each type of ken or fist), you will be in great shape.

Falls

Hoshin falls allow you to safely dissipate the impact of a fall. Falls should be quiet, relaxed, and always accompanied by a good exhale.

Side Falls - Fall to the side as the leg you are falling toward is swung in front of your weighted leg. Make contact with the ground and slide the impact out along your forearm. Remember to get low on your weighted leg as you start to fall. This minimizes the impact.

Back Fall - Fall along the back of your shoulders. Tuck your chin, roll your back, sit on your butt, and roll up the energy with a rocking motion. Exhale as your shoulders hit.

Face Fall - Fall facedown and turn your head to either side. Slide your forearms above your head with your elbows farther forward than your shoulders. Make contact with your forearms and slide.

Baby Fall - Watch how babies fall. They seldom get hurt. When you feel your balance go, go with it. Just sit down. The closer you get to the ground before actually falling, the less likely you are to get hurt. As you practice your falls, practice feeling the contact between your body and the ground. Don't think, just feel. You should be able to tell where your body touched the ground.

Earth Belt

The first kyu grade after white is Earth or Red Belt. The Earth attitude is relaxed and happy acceptance of the situation as it is. You are steady and confident. There is no feeling of danger or threat. You deal with the situation with minimal effort and motion. The chakra related to Earth is located at the tip of the tail bone. The color associated with this chakra is red. Our Earth center is the connection with the physical world.

The core strategy and body dynamics are studied to achieve the appropriate emotional reaction when threatened. This can be as simple as a conversation or as severe as being mugged. We include verbal taijutsu which is the use of elemental dynamics in conversation. Basic methods of punching, kicking, throwing and grappling are learned with attention to maximizing what your body type can do. Students are introduced to weapons such as the knife, rope or chain and hanbo. There are basically 3 kinds of weapons; Flexible, non-flexible and projectile. Weapons are used as extensions of the body. The core strategy of Hoshin Jutaijutsu has 5 basic principles.

1. The first is the universal guard. This is made by extending your arms out in front of you with your fingertips touching. The hands are rounded like you are holding a ball between the palms and point at the attackers face. The elbows are slightly bent. The hands can be lifted up or down, while keeping the fingers pointing at the opponent's center line. This shape allows students to deflect or redirect incoming attacks. Practice stepping to the side using one arm in the same guard position. The other arm is held close to the body, with the hand near your throat to protect you from any other attacks. Punches and kicks can be guided away from their intended target.

2. The next is the use of distance appropriate body weapons. The body's weapons are used depending on what weapon is within range of the opponent. The weapons are, in order from longest to shortest; Kicks, punches, knees, elbows and head. A way to practice this concept is to first kick at a target, then punch with the same side arm as you put your kicking leg down, then knee strike with the opposite side knee, then elbow with the same side elbow and lastly head butt. This sequence of body weapons can be used to close distance with an opponent. It also allows you to back out of a fight safely. Instead of using perfect footwork, attack the opponent with whatever is closest.

3. The next principle is continuous and returning fist. This is the idea of continuing to attack an opponent after your first movement. Here is a basic technique to demonstrate this: After slipping an attack, strike into their chin with your fist. Step toward them and elbow strike into the neck with the same arm as your punching fist. After your elbow strike passes their neck, with the same elbow strike in the opposite direction. Continue your motion and back fist then with the same side hand. You are getting 4 strikes to their 1. The general rule is when a weapon passes a target, it changes direction.

The legs can do the same thing. Kicks can move into knee strikes. Knees can turn into stomps on the lower leg. Kicks in Hoshin are usually doing 1 of 2 things. Either pushing through the person, like breaking down a door or attacking muscle or bone to injure or take down the opponent. Floating a kick after it makes contact enables you to decide what your next move will be. Practice stepping diagonally forward outside of a punch. With the rear leg, lightly kick your training partner's leg. After the kick makes contact, float your foot just above where it hit. There are more choices available to you. You can step on them and take them to the floor or you can slide your foot to new targets. Try kicking the upper leg, then floating your foot to the knee. Depending on how you feel, you can imagine the possibilities.

4. Next is the wedging principle. After evading the initial attack, your body moves in to take control of the opponent's weight by taking their space. Step in as you use the above principle and you will set yourself up for many types of strikes, locks and throws. Two bodies cannot occupy the same space and since you are in motion, you will have the ability to take the person off balance.

5. Lastly there is the concept of ending the fight by winning it. This is your takedown, finish, pin or knock out, depending on how you feel or how escalated the situation is. It is important to train your body and mind to finish a conflict. After you take control, get your opponent to an immobilized position or apply pain until you get a tap out. This will keep you from holding back in a real situation. Be safe with your training partners but simulate real dynamics as much as you can. These strategies are not always used in order. They are principles that can be applied when needed. If you are attacked and your guard comes up, punch to the face, then elbow as you wedge in and the guy gets knocked out... the fight is over.

In a real fight the intensity of the moment creates a certain dynamic that for the most part is a sensory overload. When a person attacks, they usually believe their strike is going to work. If it doesn't they might pause briefly before their next move. Their brain says, "Oh shit! I missed!" This moment in time is when you should practice moving into a safe position or counter strike. Move between the beats of the attacker's first move and their next. Don't block then pause. Attack just after their attack and take control of their weight. Play with this. It allows you to relax more when you train. The more intense the attack is, the longer the split second pause between their moves become. Take advantage of the time between beats. For the musicians out there, this is attacking on the upbeat.

Too often I see martial artists playing at dojo practice speed only. It works for practicing fundamentals but will not develop your instinctual reaction in a real situation. Once you get the basics down, speed up the attack. Watch how the body reacts to more intention. Stop and look where you moved to. Are you too far away? Practice stepping to the appropriate distance over and over against a fast strike. Techniques in Hoshin will not work if you don't trust their efficiency. The only way to get that is to practice so you get used to the fast attacks and can react just as easily and relaxed as you do to slow ones.

Earth Techniques

The posture of the Earth attitude is calm and relaxed. The shoulders are down, the back is straight, the head erect with the chin pulled slightly in. The knees and toes are turned out a bit. The center of Earth movement is the tip of the tail bone. Earth motion is primarily up and down movements with shifts of the hips to one side or short steps to get off the center line. The Godai breathing dynamic is slow inhale, slow exhale. Here are a few examples of Earth movements:

1. *Little misses.* As an attack is coming you shift your weight on your hips. This allows the blow to miss you slightly, giving you a safe but close proximity with which to counter. This strategy works against any attack where you don't feel threatened. Obvious follow up techniques will be easy to see. You are taking control of the weight of your attacker.
2. Against a grabbing attack. When you are grabbed in the Earth attitude you don't back away. From a grab to the lapel or chest: Cover the grabbing hand and pull to attach to yourself. Turn your whole body while staying in the same area or shifting your weight. This will allow you to take control of the weight of your attacker and use an up and then down motion to lock their wrist and take them to the floor or a knee. If grabbed from the wrist, cover and use a down and then up motion to take the attacker off balance, or an up then down motion to free you from the grab.

Earth Feeling Meditation

Imagine yourself standing on the side of a mountain. You feel the firm rock under your feet. In front of you see a wall of rock that goes way up above you. You walk over and lay your hands on the rock wall. You feel the cool, rough rock against your hands, realizing how solid and immoveable it is. You give a slight push just for fun, knowing the rock won't move. You smile. This is the feeling of Earth. Allow this feeling to fill your body. Steady and confident.

Water Belt

Water Belt is the next kyu grade in Hoshin Jutaijutsu. The Water attitude is defensive. It is moving away while gaining a safe position to strike or counter strike. The Water chakra is located at the hara, 2 inches below the navel. Its color is orange. It is associated with our emotional reactions to the world around us. The adrenal glands sit atop the kidneys and are activated when a situation becomes intense. The fight/flight response is tied into the Water center. The Godai breathing dynamic is slow inhale, fast exhale. The movements are based on fear or surprise. We usually refer to it as having guts or doing something even when you're afraid. Because the endocrine gland connected to this chakra is the adrenal glands, this level teaches your body how to channel the energy of reactive terror into power.

The Water posture is one of moving away while still maintaining the ability to retaliate from a safer position. The posture of Ichimonji no Kamae of Bujinkan Ninpo is the best physical manifestation of this attitude. The legs are spread wide for balance with the back foot making an L shape. The hips are lowered and the knees are relaxed. One hand covers the center line of the upper body, throat and solar plexus. The other is extended loosely to fend and ward off grabbing attacks. The 45 degree back angling step of the legs away from the attacker allows the individual using this posture to be completely safe from attack even though they appear vulnerable. It is like a wave wearing down a rock by flowing out and back. You move like a stream flowing around your opponent filling every opening with your presence in order to unbalance and wear them down. Water movement is constant. If you pour water onto the ground, it doesn't hit the ground, stop, move some more and then stop again. It continues to flow. This is the key to effective defensive counter attacks.

Defensive Techniques

1. As punch is approaching step back at a 45 degree angle. Swing your lead hand up to strike the attacking arm. Rock your body forward over your knee to deliver a follow up strike with the same arm.
2. Same as number one except the follow up strike is done with your rear hand while stepping forward with your rear leg. These techniques will work inside or outside the line of attack.

Instead of an uncontrolled reaction to sudden attacks, an appropriate response is practiced with real fear of danger. Water movement is typically evasive and uses 45 degree angles in defense and counter attacks. Students are taught to make distance and assess the situation. Fear is harnessed and conditioned into an effective defense.

Here is a drill to practice gaining control of your fight/flight response and Water chakra:

Stand in the middle of an open area or room. Close your eyes or use a blind fold if you think you may cheat. Have a friend or training partner walk in a circle around you at least 8 feet away. This will put them outside the normal comfort zone.

The person circling will imagine attacking the defender then touch or grab them quickly. The attacker is trying to scare or startle the defender. Observe what is happening. After repeated startles, the body will stop overreacting. Next begin moving away from the direction of the attack as you are touched. Practice stepping away from danger. Once you get a bit of control try training your footwork so the body is conditioned to react correctly. This concept can be used to get a real life feel for techniques. Realism in the dojo prepares students for the real thing. This drill will allow you to settle your fight/flight response during intense training, allowing you to retrain your instinctive reaction into a strategic reaction to danger. This replaces the natural fear reaction, which is usually to raise the hands up and tighten the body. If a real situation arises, your trained responses will emerge.

It is dangerous to think that slowly practiced techniques will suddenly turn into full speed and effective defenses during a real fight. If realistic dynamics are not practiced the students will not become accustomed to how they will react for real. If you want to know if something works, test it. Better in the dojo then on the street where your attacker may not have a regard for your safety or life. Dynamics are much more important than technical skill. Knowing your body's ability is the only way to trust your martial art. Play hard and safe.

Water Feeling Meditation
Picture yourself sitting on the beach. You look out at the ocean and notice the waves moving and flowing in toward the sand. As the waves crash against the shore you hear the sound of their power. You notice that the sound of the waves never stops. You watch as the water draws up and crashes down again. This is the feeling of water. Constantly moving to flow with and adapt to the changing situation.

Fire Belt
Fire Belt is the next kyu grade in Hoshin Jutaijutsu. The Fire chakra is located at the solar plexus. The color of this chakra is yellow. The Godai breathing dynamic is fast inhale, fast exhale. When one moves from the Fire center, there is a one pointed focus. A person will move directly through the danger or find the fastest way to resolve the conflict. This is where you,

"Joyfully leap toward the sword!" and feel excited about winning. Fire Belt covers basic Dim Mak (pressure point fighting) and advanced anatomy for combat application. Advanced weapons techniques as well as firearms are learned at this level. Students are taught to finish a fight immediately. Pain control and application are fine tuned so that fighting becomes easier. Fire Belt is about facing and overcoming obstacles.

The attitude of the Fire is directed intention. It is a "Go for it/take no prisoners!" attitude. Fire movements go right in and take control. The attacker is beat as he makes his attack. Fire is an energy releasing element. The breathing is faster and higher in the chest. You feel yourself fill with intensity as you move in to defeat your attacker. Fire is related to being excited, elated, joyous and ready to go. The negative aspect of Fire is anger. Sometimes a person is so angry that their natural fear instinct causes them to attack. This is like a snake that becomes agitated and afraid by your presence and finally strikes.

Part of the Fire Belt test is a fire walk. Doc liked to incorporate a little Japanese magic into the walk by doing a basic Gomo wish ceremony. With intent, you write a goal or ambition on a piece of wood called a konji stick. Something you would be willing to walk fire to get. After everyone walks the bed of coals the pieces of wood are thrown into the fire, symbolically releasing them into the universe. I have seen folks leap and scream as they passed over the hot coals. Sometimes their konji stick doesn't burn. Could be a sign that their goals are a ways off. After your konji is thrown into the fire, it should not be tampered with. Don't force your will on the universe. Be appreciative, driven and willing to sacrifice to reach your goals.

Break Balance

From a front choke, move forward and slide your palm over the attackers shoulder. Pull or slap behind their waist or leg with your other hand as you move forward, turning your attacker around and throwing him off balance. This can be done on opposite sides or on one side of the attacker.

Leg Lever

The leg lever can be used against any attack. You move in towards the attacker and hook your foot around their ankle. Rock your leg forward with your knee against their leg to cause pain and push them off balance. This can be done against punching, grabbing and kicking techniques. Forward movement is the key to getting a good set up on the attacker.

Hair Pull / Head Winding Takedown

Grabbing hair and twisting allows you to take an attacker in whatever direction you choose. Your other hand can be used to grab the opposite side of the persons head. Turning their head will pull them off balance making them easy to throw or take down.

Pressure Points

Certain areas of the body can be attacked in order to cause pain. In Hoshin we have a complete system of pressure point fighting techniques. Hoshin Dim Mak teaches these points, their location and ways of attacking. Below are a few of the points that are usually accessible in most street confrontations.

1. The back of the hands. The hands can be attacked with knuckles against grabs. Hitting the back of the hand may cause the motor function to be lost. If a person has a weapon this can make them drop or release it.
2. Eyes. The eyes can be poked with a finger, a knuckle, a thumb or just an open palm. Causes extreme pain, loss of sight and can be fatal if penetrated deeply enough.
3. Sternum. The sternum can be hit or you can press into it with your thumb or knuckle to cause pain. This area disrupts the electrical system and weakens the immune system.
4. Clavicle. Hooking your fingers over the clavicle and pressing down causes pain and makes the person loose strength in their legs.

5. <u>Just below the nose</u>. Strike with palm under an attackers chin. Hook fingers over the face to get one under the nose. Press in and down.
6. <u>Knee</u>. The knee can be kicked or hit with your own knee. Hit from the sides or from the top then down.
7. <u>Instep</u>. The instep can be stomped with the foot or heel. This can injure the foot and or break it, making it hard for an attacker to stand or run.
8. <u>Groin</u>. The groin area can be attacked with your knees or kicked with the shins. An attack to the groin will usually cause extreme pain, nausea and sometimes difficulty breathing.

Fire Feeling Meditation

Picture yourself sitting in front of a raging fire. You feel the heat on your face and body. The flames dance and spark, flickering yellow and orange. You reach your hands out to the fire and notice that the heat intensifies on your hand. You realize that you cannot move your hands too close to the flames or it will burn. The fire is releasing energy. This is the Fire feeling. Using explosive power to overcome your attacker, you move directly through danger to get to the fastest resolution in a conflict.

Wind Belt

The Wind or Green Belt is the next belt in Hoshin Jutaijutsu. The Wind attitude is accepting and receiving. The Wind chakra is located at the heart. Its color is lime green. The Godai breathing dynamic is fast inhale, slower exhale. Wind relates to compassion, caring and healing. The attitude is one of not wanting to harm your attacker. You are using the least amount of effort possible. The movements are light, yet very powerful and usually circular or floating to the sides moving horizontally. Wind can also be like a hurricane. You blend with your attackers movements in order to take control or avoid the attack.

The Wind Belt trains students to successfully counter most basic martial arts techniques. Students learn to deal with multiple attackers without running out of steam. Advanced anatomy and Dim Mak are studied with attention to learning to heal. Basic healing techniques are learned such as Reiki, Therapeutic Touch, massage and body work. Wind Belts are encouraged to run a shibu training group under the guidance of their Sensei. Teaching the basics deepens the instructors understanding of Hoshinjutsu techniques. Wind Belts may test students up to Fire Belt. Usually, if you are feeling compassion for someone who's attacking you, you will not want to hurt them. Shifting and turning to the side allows attacks to move right past you. Holding your arms out to the sides or up in front of you allows you to guide attacks away or hook inside of the attackers arms. You can redirect the person or allow their momentum to assist you in throwing them. Aikido is an example of a Wind martial art.

Take Downs
1. As a punch approaches shift your weight to the outside while lifting your arms. Hook the punch and step behind the person with the same side leg. Take down.
2. Same technique as number 1 except the attacker is grabbing you. Works the same but you can grab with both hands to take them down.
3. Outside wrist lock. As punch is approaching, twist your upper body to allow the punch to pass. Slide your lead hand along their arm and grab their hand. Twist in the opposite direction of your first twist. This can break their wrist, arm or shoulder and is an easy way to throw someone.

Wind Feeling Meditation
Picture yourself standing in a meadow. The grass is tall and flows gently in the breeze. You look up and see the trees along the meadow moving and swinging in the wind. You listen and hear the gusts getting stronger then almost disappearing.

You feel the gusts of air moving around your body and face. You look up and notice a leaf floating in the wind. See how the air makes the leaf seem to dance as if it were being gently guided along. This is the Wind feeling; floating in and around danger. Imagine the frustration of trying to catch a breeze. This is how your attacker will feel; as if they are fighting empty space.

Void Belt

The Blue Belt in Hoshinbudoryu is the kyu grade after Wind. This belt indicates that the student has gained significant control over his or her esoteric abilities. The main focus of this belt is the continued mastery of meditation. The advanced use of intent, Psionics, Hoshin Tao Chi Kung, knowledge of the body's meridians, fighting with energy and an array of other esoteric practices are also studied in more depth. The student is encouraged to continue their inward journey and is tested by the sensei to prove the development of these abilities. The Void Belt, which was Purple Belt in the original manuals, is where one needed to get serious about Chi Kung. As more people practiced Hoshin, it became apparent that though folks were learning the Chi Kung methods, not all were practicing enough to get the results. Later, this became an honorary belt for esoteric accomplishment outside of the Hoshinroshiryu. The kyu grades then went from Wind (Green) to Shodan (Black). Hoshin Tao Chi Kung became more of an area to study at the student's discretion. It was/is hoped that the students will practice their internal training and surpass the lower belt requirements. I feel that Chi Kung is the heart of Hoshin. In Hoshinbudoryu, you cannot get a Black Belt without developing chi.

Void in the Godai represents the 3 chakras of the throat, 3rd eye and crown collectively. The throat chakra is related to verbal communication which is probably why most people's auras are light blue. The 3rd eye is the chakra related to subtle energy awareness and spiritual knowledge. It is the portal that allows us to perceive intention empathically. Moving from the void in Hoshin Jutaijutsu refers to instinctive reaction. It's how a person reacts in a real fight, when caught off guard. By practicing the Godai elemental attitudes and techniques you can internalize them into natural, instinctive reactions. Void training involves building extra sensory awareness and the ability to sense danger or tension arising in a conflict. The state of mind referred to as Mushin or no-mind reflects the void attitude. Not having to think, just reacting instinctively to a situation.

When you move from the Void centers your movements will be spontaneous. You won't realize what you are doing until it has already occurred. Meditation combined with the physical techniques will bring together your mind, body and spirit or intention. All parts of you working together, giving the best response possible. Your response should be driven by your emotions which relate to the chakra centers.

Sensitivity Training

Developing a 6th sense or the ability to perceive danger is part of the training in Hoshin and old school Ninpo. Blindfolded training is used to become sensitive to oncoming danger. Start by having a training partner walk toward you slowly. As they get closer have them reach for your face. If you think you feel them coming, raise your hand. If you are correct, your partner should tap you on the raised hand. Practice this exercise with your back to your partner. With time you will be able to perceive the attack coming almost all of the time. Have your partner use different attitudes as you do this exercise. Try to tell what the "feeling" of your attacker is. Are they scared, nervous, angry or running up to tell you good news? Remember how each of your partners attitudes felt. This will help you develop the ability to discern different emotions. After this exercise is mastered, move on to multiple attackers. These exercises are lots of fun and help bring your attention to the present moment.

External Awareness Meditation

Get into your meditative posture and begin belly breathing. As you inhale, imagine you are drawing energy into your body. As you exhale, imagine that a bubble is forming around you. You can breathe in energy and fill this bubble by exhaling. Imagine that the bubble is getting bigger. Start out with a bubble just a few feet wide. Pay attention to a particular area within the bubble, for example the area to your left side. Move around to different areas in your bubble, spending a few moments to become aware of your surroundings. Later, have a friend walk slowly toward you from any direction. See if you can notice where they penetrate your bubble. With time you will become sensitive to anything entering your zone. Women have a predisposition to this ability. It is a natural part of their built in defense mechanism. You may find yourself moving away from doors that are suddenly opened or ducking something flying past your head. This is your subconscious mind helping to keep you out of harm's way.

Death Meditation

This meditation is simple and will bring your mind to mushin. Imagine you have one minute left to live. Think about how you feel. What is important? If you truly think that you will die in one minute your mind will shift to being in your last few moments. Your senses will come alive and you will feel yourself in the present moment. Mushin.

Shodan (1st Degree Black Belt)

This is the first Black Belt rank in Hoshinbudoryu Jutaijutsu. The student must be able to teach all techniques through Blue Belt. Students must achieve the lesser Kan and Li (opening of the Microcosmic Orbit). Usually a Blue Belt teaches for one year to qualify for Shodan. The techniques learned for Shodan ensure the student will not only be competent in the Godai attitude for each of the five elements, but will also learn ways to successfully counter these strategies.

Students practice advanced, realistic Jutaijutsu against multiple attackers, both armed and unarmed. A Black Belt in Hoshin learns to counter all Hoshin Jutaijutsu techniques and the kihon Happo of Bujinkan Budo Taijutsu. Advanced weapons training and espionage are also studied. Using only kamae and breath the student must demonstrate the ability to stop any throw in Hoshinjutsu. They should also be able to shield themselves from mental manipulation or at least be able to keep functioning while under attack, mental or physical. Students learn to defend themselves from disadvantaged positions such as sitting in a chair or handcuffed or bound at the wrists.

Living Philosophy
In their own words, students must demonstrate a complete knowledge of the oral traditions as well as the physical techniques by breaking down exactly what goes into each level and what is added or taken away at each belt.

Nidan (2nd Degree Black Belt)
Nidan is the second degree Black Belt in Hoshinjutsu. If you have not by now, you must solve your koan or riddle and contribute an original variation or totally new technique to the system. You must write and lead directed meditations that manifest the following elementals: Earth, Water, Fire, Wind, Void, Intention and Healing.

Students practice advanced meditation for developing the ability to externalize chi. Empty force training is learned at this level. Techniques for astral projection and remote viewing are also learned. The esoteric Godai Kata is practiced to further strengthen the energy levels in the body and keep the chakras balanced. The dynamics of Systema are incorporated into the physical training.

"Systema" (Russian Martial Art)
These techniques are drawn from the Russian system of combat known as Systema or "the system". It is an ancient

form of combat. After the communist takeover of Russia, the new government outlawed traditional Russian martial arts. They did however realize the effectiveness of the ancient system and kept it secret from the general public. Only the elite Special Forces or Spetsnaz were taught the system. After the fall of communism in Russia, the old system was brought out of hiding. This system is headed in North America by Vladimir Visiliev. He is an ex-special operations unit soldier who fought in high risk missions during the Russian conflict in Afghanistan. He also served as a bodyguard for high ranking Russian Military leaders and was a trainer of the elite Russian Special Forces.

There are no ranks or belts in Systema, only practice and improvement. Systema is an incredible art which has loose, adaptive movements. The body moves on a rotating central axis. The legs twist to allow you to retain your balance when attacked. The arms use circular, whipping motions to deliver incredibly powerful strikes. Techniques for absorbing and redirecting the energy of strikes are learned and are done in a completely relaxed manner. The body and mind are worked intensively to overcome fear and build confidence. I found it interesting that all of the elemental dynamics are incorporated at the same time in their motion. The focus of the eyes is above the head to connect with the universal energy. The attitude used in the system is loving compassion for your enemy.

The basic stance that is used in the system is similar to the Shizen no Kamae of Ninpo and Hoshin. The arms are turned in a bit more and the legs are loose. The system uses the concept of constant motion. This is a bit difficult for those trained in traditional Asian martial arts. There is no pause between movements. The body is allowed to move in whatever direction it has to so strikes and blows can slip by. Keep your legs loose so you can easily twist and rotate to absorb attacks. This will also give you the ability to counter as you evade/absorb the attack. Use a loose swinging motion of the arms when striking. The arm strikes swing in circular or figure eight patterns and are combined with elbow strikes as you get close. Here are a few Systema based techniques to play with:

1. Swing your left arm out and turn your wrist down as you roll your shoulder inward to whip your arm to the right, striking with the back of your hand. Rotate your wrist to the left as you whip the back of your hand in the opposite direction. Swing right arm out while turning it inward as well. As it completes the inward slap turn it over to hook in a clockwise direction to outward swat, then slap with the left arm using a diagonal swat. Play with it and you will feel how each strike leads into the next. Do this slowly at first then learn to whip them quickly.

2. (Against a punch) Turn inward, cover your face and leaning back a bit; your opposite side leg rotates outward to keep your balance. You can cover your face as you are attacked and it will block the punches from hitting you. Use a brushing motion like you are wiping your face off. Try it out.

3. (Against a punch) As the punch is coming at you, lift your arm up and out to make contact with your forearm to the punching arm. Fold your arm to absorb the punch, rotate your elbow so you can circle around the punching arm and strike to the attacker by extending your same side hand to their face.

Pushing exercises allow a person to eliminate fear of being caught off guard as well as build sensitivity. The object should be to go with the force of your attacker. Pushes should be to shoulders, hips and knees. Practice pushes from the front and from behind. If you are shoved very hard from behind you can lift your leg to hook around the attacker's leg or body. This will stop their motion. You should also practice with a training knife to your back.

The shoulders and head can be used to redirect or absorb strikes as well. Practice deflecting blows outward and inward. Use the rotation of your shoulder to catch the punch. You can also deflect a shot with your head by relaxing and turning your neck to let your head rotate away from the punch. Hook chin over his wrist, step in and throw or takedown.

You can also stop an attack by letting the assailant run into your fist. Step in and place your fist on the side or the attackers face just like you would be hitting him. Keep elbow bent like a cross punch or the universal guard. Another fun technique is to step outside of a punch while pushing on the opposite shoulder of the punching arm. This will twist the attacker around. You can pull them into you to take down.

Esoteric Godai Kata

This exercise is extremely beneficial. Practicing this exercise will assist in giving flow to your technique execution as well as speed the process of Kundalini arousal or Greater Kan and Li. Once Kundalini has been awakened, this practice will keep meridians open and lessen side effects of chi sickness. The movements are those of the San Shin no Kata of Ninpo. If you don't know them, there are tons of videos on Youtube or Bujinkan training DVDs. Practicing the San Shin in this manner will connect the movements to an elemental centers corresponding emotion. Use the proper breathing dynamics for each element and align the movements to your breath.

1. Earth Kata - Move chi to Earth chakra. Pat pubic bone. Cover with your hands. Picture red energy and open the base chakra. Perform Earth Kata with proper attitude and breath.
2. Water Kata - Move chi to Water chakra. Pat Dan Tien. Cover with hands and picture orange energy at the navel. Open the Water chakra. Perform Water Kata with proper attitude and breath.
3. Fire Kata - Move chi to the Fire chakra. Pat solar plexus. Cover with hands and picture yellow energy. Open the Fire chakra. Perform Fire Kata with proper attitude and breath.
4. Wind Kata - Move chi to Wind chakra. Swirl hand over the heart and picture green energy. Open the wind chakra. Perform Wind Kata with proper attitude and breath.

5. Void Kata - Move chi to head. Tap your third eye, then center of forehead at the hair line and crown. Look up at the third eye and picture violet. With a small, circular motion, rub the third eye. Look further up into top of head. Picture the color indigo fading into white. Rub the center of forehead head and crown. Perform Void Kata in Mushin.

Once all of the sections have been learned and the Shodan has taught for at least 9 months, they will qualify to test for Nidan. They must demonstrate their original technique or variation of a martial principle. They must show the ability to handle random fight scenarios (randori). They must also pass the sakki test (sword avoidance while kneeling in meditation) for promotion to Nidan in Hoshin Jutaijutsu.

After Nidan, the student continues to run their training group and works on mastery of Hoshin Healing or another healing modality. In Hoshin, the Sandan (3rd degree black belt) is the level one is expected to achieve Hoshin Healer certification. The 4th and 5th degree Black Belts were Shihan level in traditional Hoshinroshiryu Jutaijutsu. The title Roshi (spirit master) was used by Glenn for instructors at these ranks. Traditionally, once a Black Belt reached Godan they were expected to go off and do their own thing. This was the point in which you became the master of your own expression of the art.

After Glenn passed, I decided that our system would add additional Black Belt ranks in order to show continued learning and development. I have included the criteria that our ryu uses for the dan ranking. These are the guidelines for the Yudansha (Black Belt members) in Hoshinbudoryu. This format ensures the teacher is successfully mentoring their students while continuing to work on themselves.

Black Belt Rank Requirements

Shodan (1st)
Able to teach White- Void Belt Hoshinjutsu
Teach training group or privately for 6-8 months
Pass Shodan test

Nidan (2nd)
Able to teach White- Shodan Hoshinjutsu
Add a new technique or variation to the physical system (jutaijutsu)
Teach training group or privately another 8 months
Pass Nidan test

Sandan (3rd)
Certified Hoshin Healer
Teach training group or privately another 8 months
Have 2 Earth belt students or 1 Fire belt

Yondan (4th)
Teach training group or privately another 8 months – 1 year
Complete training in ryu course of your choice
Have 2 Water belt students or 1 Wind belt
Host Soke or another Hoshinbudoryu instructor seminar and/or visit hombu once a year or attend Hoshinfest.

Godan (5th)
Teach training group or privately another 8 months – 1 year
Complete training in ryu course of your choice **or** achieve dan rank in another system
Add a new concept to the Hoshin system
Have 2 Fire belt students or 1 Shodan
Host Soke or another Hoshinbudoryu instructor seminar and/or visit hombu once a year or attend Hoshinfest.

Rokudan (6th)
Teach training group or privately another 8 months- 1 year
Complete training for **Instructor** level in either: Hoshin Tao Chi Kung, Mandala Therapy or Hoshin Healing
Have 2 Wind belt students or 1 Nidan
Host Soke or another Hoshinbudoryu instructor seminar and/or visit hombu once a year or attend Hoshinfest.

Shichidan (7th)
Teach training group or privately another 8 months- 1 year
Complete training for **Instructor** level in either: Hoshin Tao Chi Kung, Mandala Therapy, Hoshin Healing, Psionics or Mikkyo
Have 2 Shodan students or 1 Sandan
Host Soke or another Hoshinbudoryu instructor seminar and/or visit hombu once a year or attend Hoshinfest.

Hachidan (8th)
Awaken Kundalini (Greater Kan and Li)
Familiar with **all** areas of Hoshin budo ryu
Teach training group or privately another 1 year
Complete training for **Instructor** level in additional area: Hoshin Tao Chi Kung, Mandala Therapy, Hoshin Healing, Psionics or Mikkyo
Have 2 Nidan students or 1 Yondan
Host Soke or another Hoshinbudoryu instructor seminar and/or visit hombu once a year or attend Hoshinfest.

Kyudan (9th)
Teach training group or privately another 1 year
Complete training for **Instructor** level in additional area:
Hoshin Tao Chi Kung, Mandala Therapy, Hoshin Healing, Psionics or Mikkyo
Have 2 Sandan students or 1 Godan
Host Soke or another Hoshinbudoryu instructor seminar and/or visit hombu once a year or attend Hoshinfest.
* *must have written nominations from 2 dan ranking ryu members*

Judan (10th)
Write a book or manuscript on Hoshin/Hoshin related concepts or area of your choice
Teach training group or privately another 1 year
Complete training for **Instructor** level in additional area: Hoshin Tao Chi Kung, Mandala Therapy, Hoshin Healing, Psionics, Hoshin Mikkyo or KAP.
Continue to supervise your network of students and instructors
Host Soke or another Hoshinbudoryu instructor seminar and/or visit hombu once a year
* *must have written nominations from 3 dan ranking ryu members*

Combat martial arts of old had one thing in common. Their purpose was to keep the warriors alive and to win against enemy strategy and technique. The intense, daily, rigorous training of old has since been replaced by traditional kata based on the methods of the originators of martial systems. Most of today's martial arts are a shadow of the ancient past where techniques decided life or death. The intense physical training was balanced by internal exercises to counteract the stress from long hours of focused training in killing methods. Practicing killing methods can make one callous and cold.

Sport martial arts are culturally refined and remove the "My enemy must die!" mentality. In some circles, even the Bujinkan has evolved in this way. Some of the Bujinkan training is based on historical movements of Samurai wearing armor. The emotionally based reactions have less importance. I believe this is due to the fact that there are a large number of Bujinkan practitioners in the world.

The ura or hidden aspects of Ninpo have faded into the shadows. Most who are capable don't share it very often, if ever. There are still a few who openly show the magic. Dr. Morris and I would discuss this often. Hoshin was his way of being able to share the secrets of the martial arts without pissing off the Ninjas. He was given a lot of grief for detailing the hidden side effects of emotionally based training and chi development.

Where the ancient ninja lived the Tendai Mikkyo philosophy, the modern ninjas (or folks who study the ninja arts) treat Mikkyo as a less-than important aspect or briefly touched upon it in their training. I trained with older ninja folks where the Godai was the basic theory behind why each kihon worked the way it did, mechanically, bioenergetically and emotionally. This is more attributed to Steve Hayes' expression of Ninpo, but it surely did not start with him. The real Ninpo instructors are those who have trained extensively with Hatsumi and his Shihan in Japan or study with a Shidoshi that keeps up with the current stream of training. Hayes simply explained a bit of Japanese cosmology to westerners.

I hear that some Hoshin practitioners are focusing on a primarily physical system and not on the ura of Hoshin. The progression as to where it will go is obvious. Remove the underlying principles and you have a watered down version of the original system. Some learn the theory but don't practice the methods to cultivate chi or they do not understand why Glenn was so adamant about a Godai based martial art being superior. There are people showing the Earth, Water, Fire, Wind and Void concepts who don't know how they relate or the way proper dynamics are achieved when using the Godai. Again, shadows of the original. The esoteric aspects of Hoshin cannot be separated from the physical system. It was designed that way, though most never trained enough to get it. I see people who do "Come to Jesus" as a variation of Hon Gyaku from Ninpo. The Hoshin electrical application is much different. You have to have chi to make Hoshin Jutaijutsu work correctly. Period. Otherwise you are mimicking the real art. If folks continue to mimic what they think Hoshin is, it will be no different of an evolution than other once esoteric systems of martial arts.

Chapter 3

Hoshin Healing

When I walked in for my acceptance interview at the Southeastern School of Neuromuscular and Massage Therapy, the director, Janice Schulke, greeted me with a big smile and a warm hand shake. I noticed that every time she asked me a question and I answered, she would shift her eyes to the sides and top of my head. After I explained why I thought I would do well in her school, she looked at me puzzled and said "You have a lot of energy! What have you been doing?" I explained Hoshin and Dr. Morris' Chi Kung. Janice was a Reiki master, an ex EMT and nurse. She was quite the adrenalin junkie who used to repel from helicopters into the thick Carolina mountain forests to rescue hikers. She is about 5' 2" but can get the toughest knots out. She was the massage therapist for the Carolina Panthers.

The first day of class Janice and the other students, mostly women, were in the back of the classroom chatting. I walked into the class and Janice (whose back was to me across the room) turned around and looked at me smiling. I walked over to greet everyone and introduced myself. Janice said she was glad I was in class. The curriculum was incredible. Aside from the standard neuromuscular therapy, anatomy and physiology, Swedish and therapeutic massage, Janice would bring in instructors on an array of healing modalities and specialties. I learned myofascial release (MFR), clinical aromatherapy, lymphatic drainage, pre-natal massage, Reflexology, Usui Reiki, Therapeutic Touch, European hot stone massage, acupressure, Thai massage, ear candling and much more. She asked my help in teaching Chinese medicine theory to the class. I taught Jin Shin Jutsu, Hoshin Tao Chi Kung, and women's self-protection. I am forever grateful for the knowledge I gained from her.

I created the Hoshin Healing system at the request of Dr Morris. Traditionally in Hoshin to get Sandan (3rd degree), you had to earn a certification in massage or any other healing modality. Glenn said "Folks go outside our system to get their healing certification from someone else. I want our ryu to have a complete healing system. You are a healer. Make it happen."

Glenn asked me to create a system that could be taught through distance training. I filmed DVDs of all the physical methods and wrote the Hoshin Healing manual. Hoshin Healing techniques are drawn from the best techniques I learned and used in my practice as a professional massage therapist. The methods are what worked the best and made performing massage easier. The system is similar to the structure of Hoshinjutsu. There are 4 levels with a certification and Hoshin Healing instructor program available. The following information comes from the Hoshin Healing manual:

Western thought has always regarded the mind and body as separate entities. A holistic approach means recognizing that the mind and the spirit have a direct, powerful effect on how the body functions. Natural therapies are much older than Western treatments such as surgery and antibiotics. Herbal remedies have been around for at least 5,000 years. In fact, 'homeopathy' was as big as 'allopathy' as late as the early nineteenth century. There were dozens of eclectic medical colleges in the nineteenth century, which taught an approach to medicine that ultimately became naturopathy, a type of medicine that uses a number of alternative techniques, including homeopathy, acupuncture, massage, hydrotherapy, herbal therapy and vitamin therapy. The naturopaths treat not only the disorder, but seek to affect the cause. For example, instead of prescribing an antibiotic to wipe out an infection, a naturopathic physician might prescribe a combination of natural remedies to attack the infection. Then will try to determine which factors in the patient's daily life, such as stress, poor nutrition, or inadequate exercise are the root causes of the disorder. One area where alternative treatment is particularly helpful is the managing of stress, which has been implicated in a wide range of conditions from allergies to gastrointestinal disorders and heart disease.

Interest in natural healing has been increasing since the 1960's. It stems from a combination of the anti-establishment movement and President Nixon's 1974 visit to China, which led to loosening of immigration laws for people from the East. Today, people are seeking to take more control of their destinies in personal and family health issues. This is being fueled by the rising cost of health insurance, treatment, and prescription medications. Further, conventional medicine does not do well with chronic illnesses. This explains why they are chronic. These include chronic fatigue syndrome, arthritis and irritable bowel syndrome.

More people are attracted to the alternative emphasis on treating the whole person - mind, body, and spirit. The main reason for the failure of modern medicine is that it is dealing with results and not causes. True healing involves treating the cause of the suffering, physical, mental and emotional. When emotional and psychological stresses are stabilized, functional and other disorders (which have strong emotional and psychological components as underlying causes) often resolve themselves or can be treated more easily. It's not enough to recognize your physical symptoms. You have to get to know yourself on a deeper level.

The most basic thing you should keep in mind is, let the Earth help heal the person. You should not use your own Chi to heal. Eventually you will burn out. Exchanging energy with the recipient can cause adverse reactions if they are charged by depression or any other negative physical or mental state. Grounding is necessary so that the sick energy can pass back into the Earth. I would get stomach pains, diarrhea and headaches until I finally started letting the Earth do the work. Keep your knees slightly bent during the entire session. If your legs lock straight, energy gets trapped in your body. Negative reactions can happen very quickly, sometimes even during the session. Keep your tongue up as well. If you are doing energy work, pull cool healing energy up from the Earth. Bring it up your legs and up and out of your arms and hands. Pull sick energy off as you inhale. If you are performing massage, simply pull out the sick energy while inhaling and doing a return stroke. Send energy into them while exhaling into your massage stroke. Use a rocking, Tai Chi like motion as you perform massage. Align your breath with your movements. The key to good bodywork is keeping a smooth transition from area to area. Maintain contact with the person at all times if they are new to bodywork. This helps build trust.

In a traditional relaxation massage, it is best to start at the head and face. The sense organs are clustered on the head. Massaging the head and face allow you to gauge the trust the person has for you. Start at the head and gently massage the scalp with your fingertips. Move to the sides of the nose, cheeks and ears. Watch the person's hands. Are they clinched into a fist? Look for subtle clues as to their comfort level such as excessive tension in the arms. Gently shaking a limb will show you if you are relaxing the person.

I once had a client who would come in for relaxation massage. She was typically very tense and stiff during the previous few massages. I could lift her arm a few inches off the table and let go, only to watch it hang there in the air. At her next session I told her I was going to guide her through a visualization to help her relax. I put on a CD of ocean waves and took her through the Hoshin mental vacation meditation. She was able to relax considerably and felt much better afterward.

First Aid

First aid is defined as the immediate and temporary care given a victim of an accident or sudden illness until the services of a physician can be obtained. It relates to the victim's mind and spirit as well as to his physical injuries. Although many people study first aid in order to help others, the training primarily helps the student. First aid training also helps students to develop safety consciousness. Most accidents are minor and first aid is all that is needed. With more serious injuries, apply first aid, make the victim comfortable, and get help. (For further information obtain a book on first aid from the library or take a course in Standard First Aid and CPR).

Acupressure

Acupressure is as old as instinct. When your head hurts, you rub your temples. The goal of acupressure is the same as acupuncture, except acupressure uses fingers or hand pressure instead of needles. The goal is to stimulate the basic body energy or chi to improve healing. Acupressure is the older, original technique. However, acupressure is often more powerful than acupuncture for relieving everyday aches, pains, and stress. Another advantage of pressure over puncture is that you can do it yourself. And it's simple and cheap if you use common sense. The only thing you can do wrong is be a little too vigorous.

The basic human impulse, to touch to heal, was combined with the principles of traditional Chinese medicine about 4,000 years ago in a text titled *Yellow Emperor's Classic of Internal Medicine*. In this text, and over the next two millennia, Chinese healers discovered a system of channels and points on the body that, when correctly touched or stimulated, would relieve pain and speed healing. The Chinese healers called these channels meridians, which are invisible wires that conducted the body's chi, or energy. When these channels are disturbed or blocked, the energy flowing through them will be too fast or too slow, too turbulent or too static, and the body's chi will be unbalanced. The goal of acupressure treatment, therefore, is to restore a state of energy balance. When a person is totally healthy, physically, mentally and emotionally, energy will flow through the body freely and balanced, like electricity.

None of us are totally healthy. We all experience disease, injury, and emotional trauma. In addition there are environmental factors such as pollution and noise. Acupressure can be used to rebalance and unblock the energy that flows through your body, so that your body can begin to heal itself. The basic acupressure technique is 'use medium to firm pressure'. To apply pressure you can use your thumb, fingers, palms, or knuckles. When applying pressure with one finger, the middle finger is usually the best choice. The sensation should fall somewhere between pain and pleasure. Most acupressure points occur in symmetrical pairs. This means that one point is on the left side and one point is on the right side of your body. Both points in a pair should be pressed simultaneously when possible. To relax an area or relieve pain, first press the points gently for 30 seconds. Increase the pressure until it is firm, holding it for one to three minutes. Then release slowly and gently, again taking about 30 seconds to gradually come off the points.

When you're working on acupressure points in a large muscle group, kneading is often used before applying acupressure. Use your thumbs and fingers and the heels of your hands to knead the points as well as the areas around them before you apply direct pressure. Always be gentle. Don't "massage" a point as you are applying direct pressure. This can cause further injury. Quick tapping with the fingertips stimulates muscles that are located just under the surface of the skin. Work gently on acupressure points on sensitive parts of the body, such as the face and abdomen, or on areas where there is little cushioning between skin and bone, such as top of the head.

You do not have to be an expert or a licensed professional to use your hands as healing tools. A hug or pat on the back can be shared with family members and friends; so can acupressure. We live in a touch-deprived culture and I believe that this is one of the reasons why we have so much domestic violence and depression.

5 Minute Acupressure Workout

Like a physical workout, this routine is best done at least three days a week, although it can be done every day.

1. Begin by sitting in a chair in a comfortable position with your spine straight. Find the Sea of Vitality (points B 23 and B 47) on your lower back.
2. Place the backs of your hands along both sides of the spine. Rub briskly up and down for 30 seconds, feeling the warmth from the friction.
3. Place your middle and index finger under one side of the base of the skull, using the thumb of the same hand on the other side to gently press the 'Gates of Consciousness' (points GB 20) at the base of your skull.
4. Using the middle finger of your other hand, gently press the Third Eye for a couple of minutes before slowly releasing all points.
5. Tilt your head back comfortably, close your eyes and take three long, slow, deep breaths.
6. Keep breathing deeply as you do a quick mental survey of your body to locate tension. Let the tension stream out of your body with each exhalation until you feel your body release any tightness. Continue breathing deeply for a few minutes. With each inhalation, imagine healing energy flowing into your body. Hold the 'Sea of Energy' (point CV

6), three finger-widths below your naval on your lower abdomen. Sit straight with your shoulders relaxed. Close your eyes and press this point firmly and breathe deeply for one minute.

Meridians

There are 12 major meridians, each of which is connected to a specific organ. Six of these meridians - lung, heart, pericardium, liver, spleen and kidney - flow up the front of the body. Conversely, six meridians - small intestine, large intestine, bladder, stomach, gallbladder and triple warmer - run down the back. Another set of meridians, called the eight extraordinary channels, run through the body in routes not directly related to the major organs. Acupressure points are located along all of the meridians.

There are also two very important meridians or vessels called the Governing Channel (GV) and Conception Channel (CV). The Governing Channel runs at the base of the spine (tailbone), up the back and over the top of the head to the center of the upper lip. This channel links the spinal column, brain, and nervous system. The Conception Channel flows from the head down to the perineum (the space between the anus and genitals). It is linked to the digestive and reproductive systems.

Acupressure points are usually identified by the abbreviation of its meridian and a specific number. In Chinese medicine, the points have poetic names such as 'Sea of Tranquility,' 'Wind of Heaven,' and 'Welcoming Perfume.' For example, LI 4 means point 4 on the large intestine meridian, and St 36 is point 36 on the stomach meridian. Acupressure remedies usually combine points near the area of pain or tension with points that seem to have no obvious connection to the immediate problem. Chinese medicine refers to nearby points as local points and the faraway points as trigger points. Trigger points work because the meridian pathways connect the points.

Shorthand for the Meridians

Meridians that Flow up the Body

Abbv.	Meridian
Lu	Lung
H	Heart
P	Pericardium
Lv	Liver
Sp	Spleen
K	Kidney

Meridians that Flow Down the Body

Abbv.	Meridian
SI	Small Intestine
LI	Large Intestine
B	Bladder
St	Stomach
GB	Gallbladder
TW	Triple Warmer

Chakras

Chakra is a Sanskrit word which means wheel. The chakras are energy centers that are positioned along the central axis of the body. Chakras regulate the energy fields of the body, which generate the body's aura. The Chakras are also related the nerve nexii along the spine as well as regulate the endocrine system.

The first chakra (Muladhara) is located at the tip of the tail bone. It is associated with the earth element and is the color red. The attitude associated with Muladhara is steady confidence. This chakra also grounds you to the physical world.

The second chakra (Svadhisthana) is located approximately 2.5" below the navel, this area is called the Hara in Japanese. It is associated with the water element and is the color orange. This chakra is the seat of the emotions and relates to the fight/flight response.

The third chakra (Manipura) is located at the solar plexis. It is associated with the fire element and is the color yellow. This chakra represents the energy releasing states, i.e. excitement, adventurous, ready to take on the world.

The fourth chakra (Anahata) is located at the heart center. It is associated with the element of wind and the color is green. This chakra is related to compassion, caring, healing, etc.

The fifth chakra (Visuddha) is located at the throat center. It is associated with speech and communication and its color is blue. This chakra is the first of the higher energy centers and shows our distinction between us and the rest of creation.

The sixth chakra (Ajna) is located between the eyes just above the brow line. It is called the third eye and relates to spirituality and extra-sensory ability and its color is indigo/violet. This center is the doorway to higher spiritual awareness.

The seventh chakra (Sahasrara) is located at the crown of the head. It is associated with enlightenment and universal awareness/consciousness. Its color is white.

Chakra Diagnosis

You can test the strength of each chakra manually using simple muscle tests. Have the person you are testing extend an arm out to the side and hold. Put your hand on their arm and tell them to resist. Press down to test their arm strength (not too hard). Now hold your other hand in front of each chakra and repeat the strength test. Weaker chakras will weaken their arm while stronger ones will have greater strength. This will indicate where the energy is dominant. Looking at a list of aura colors and meanings, a quick assessment of the emotions can also be given. This may reveal the personal insecurities, weaknesses or strengths of a person.

Hoshin Tao Chi Kung practitioners and Kundalini survivors usually will feel balanced at each center with the strongest chakra being the crown. Experiment and see if you can "read" a person using this method. You may be surprised at what you can tell about someone. These diagnostics will offer greater understanding of personality and emotional tendencies. It is a way to learn where work or attention is needed.

Research has found that relaxation and meditation techniques can boost immunity, short-circuit anger, curb smoking, and relieve insomnia, back pain, high blood pressure, motion sickness, impotence and irritable bowel syndrome. It has been used to treat diabetes, psoriasis, rheumatoid arthritis, panic attacks, phobias and depression. Learning to neutralize the effects of stress is one of the most important aspects of preventive medicine.

Excessive amounts of stress can adversely affect almost every part of your body. Eighty percent of patients seen by primary care physicians have some stress-related symptoms. Overall, stress-related ailments cost American business and industry more than $100 billion annually in lost productivity and absenteeism. Consistently evoking the stress response with images of danger in the past or stress in the future is tantamount to setting off a false fire alarm in your body. Mental rest breaks can evoke the relaxation response, a physiological state that has been shown to lessen feelings of stress and anxiety. The relaxation response reduces muscle tension, lowers heart rate, blood pressure, metabolism and breathing and starts tranquil feelings. Although the relaxation response is often associated with a simple form of meditation, it may easily be conjured by other relaxation and meditation techniques.

The relaxation response blunts the release of adrenaline, catecholamine, and other stress hormones that trigger the fight-or-flight response. An overdose of stress hormones can suppress the immune system and elevate blood cholesterol levels. There are literally dozens of ways to produce the relaxation response. All of the techniques can work. It is a matter of discovering which ones work best for you. Using a combination of techniques, such as deep breathing, followed by progressive relaxation can increase the power of the relaxation effect. Each technique takes you down a level into a deeper, longer-lasting state of relaxation.

Deep breathing is one of the simplest ways to relax, and is integral with many other relaxation techniques. When you slow down your breathing and focus your attention in your lower belly (dan tien), it creates profound physiological and psychological effects. Deep abdominal breathing relaxes tight chest muscles and opens up blood vessels, so your heart can pump more efficiently. It also helps you think clearer, so you can stay relaxed in a stressful situation. Although deep breathing can literally be performed anywhere and anytime, here is a method that can be practiced as part of a regular health maintenance program:

Sit in a chair with your back straight. Slowly breathe in and feel your lungs filling from the bottom to the top. Focus your attention just below your navel. Let it expand as you breathe. It should feel like your diaphragm is being pulled down. Then slowly exhale, emptying your lungs from top to bottom. Feel the diaphragm relax into its natural position. Do this twice a day for five minutes.

Meditation is a form of mental martial arts. It helps us keep ourselves centered so that we are no longer at the mercy of our own thoughts. Probably the best known type of meditation is transcendental meditation (TM), an effortless technique introduced and taught by Maharishi Mahesh Yogi. Concentration meditation uses a picture, a word (mantra), an object or sensation to focus the mind. When your mind drifts, you refocus your attention on the object. Mindfulness meditation is more complex. Instead of focusing on a single sensation or object, you allow your thoughts, feelings, and images to float through your mind. In mindfulness, you are a dispassionate observer. You note your thoughts, desires, and sensations in the same way that a postal worker might notice stamps. You let these thoughts go in and out of your mind without expressing positive or negative feelings about them.

By systematically tightening and relaxing muscles, progressive relaxation can prevent stress from overcoming you. Developed in the 1920s by Edmund Jacobson, a Chicago physician, progressive relaxation is considered an excellent technique for beginners because it is practical and doesn't depend on imagination.

Five Relaxation Enhancers

1. Stop Smoking. Smoking triggers the release of stress hormones in the body.
2. Reduce Caffeine. Caffeine is a stimulant that can trigger the fight-or-flight response to stress.
3. Eat Carbohydrates. Eating grains, vegetables, and fruits loaded with complex carbohydrates, such as spaghetti, baked beans, and apples, can trigger the release of hormones that will help you relax.
4. Work up a sweat. Regular exercise is a fundamental part of any relaxation program. It can lower anxiety, fend off depression and help increase self-esteem. Walk 15 to 20 minutes a day.
5. Make time to laugh. Humor is a powerful ally in the quest for relaxation. A good laugh triggers the release of endorphins (chemicals in the brain that produce feelings of euphoria). It also suppresses the production of cortical (a hormone released when you are under stress that immediately raises blood pressure).

To be successful at massage therapy and energy work, the ability to feel energy blockages and spasms must be developed. The following exercises will increase these abilities:

1. This exercise increases your awareness of your own aura. Rub your palms together as if you were warming your hands. With your palms still facing each other, separate them about

8 inches apart. Slowly move them toward each other using a soft bouncing motion. You should notice a polarity between them. Slowly move them closer together until you feel them begin to pull toward each other. This is caused by the aura of each hand crossing the field of the other. Now move them away from each other until the "pulling" stops. Find the point in which the pushing away and pulling toward switches. This is the edge of your aura. As you develop more energy through meditation this distance will increase.

2. This exercise develops your ability to palpate spasms in muscles. It increases your ability to feel deep below the skin with little or no pressure. Take a strand of hair and put it under a sheet of paper. Using your fingertip or edge of your pinky finger, try to feel the hair under the paper. Continue to add more sheets until you can feel the hair through a thick pile of paper. A phone book is perfect for this exercise. Remember not to press down with your finger. Slide over the pages with a very light touch.

During energy work, align your breath with your recipient. Pull the sick energy up the arms and see it going down and out of your feet on your exhales. My best advice is to keep your intent simple. I usually just send the energy through the orbit linking the person to me and connecting to the Earth. I send neutral healing energy and allow it to go where it's needed. There may be another part of their body that needs your healing energy more than the area you are focusing on. After sending energy through the person so their body can begin healing itself, you then can focus on using energy to help a specific area or loosen knots. I don't try to make a knot release. Just imagine the healing occurring, as though you are waiting for it. The more you practice the faster it will work each time.

I once worked with a young woman who was a bit naïve but curious about energy work. She said she had kidney problems and asked if I could do anything to help her. I warmed my hands, placed them on her lower back and sent healing energy to her kidneys. A few days later she approached me at work and told me her parents wanted to thank me. I asked her what for. She explained that she had been experiencing pre-cancerous kidney failure. At her last checkup the Doctor couldn't believe he was examining the same patient. Her kidneys were working great. I believe that not knowing the severity of her illness made it easier for me to let go and allow the energy to flow. I asked what she had told her family that I had done to her. She said "I told them you used your 'cheese' to fix me." I had to laugh. It was the best healing I have ever accidentally done.

Two important concepts in massage therapy are "centering" and "grounding". Centering is based on settling yourself into an appropriate attitude for healing. This is done by becoming aware of your "Hara" (area about 2 inches below your navel). You can place your hands over this area to help bring your attention to it. Calm your mind and put unnecessary thoughts aside. Get yourself into a loving state of mind. This helps to focus your intention on healing. Grounding is based on the concept that you have a connection with the patient and you function as a conduit, helping the patient release unwanted tension and feelings of stress. Your feet are flat on the ground and knees slightly bent.

Relaxation Massage

Basic massage is primarily for relaxation. The stroke that is used is called effleurage. The purpose of the "relaxation" stroke is to apply lotion and feel for spasms, as well as warm tissues. It is a smooth "gliding stroke" that is performed using the palms. The hands are placed flat on the patient. As one hand glides along the skin, the other follows behind in a fashion similar to a train. The hands switch as they return. If your right hand is in front of your left when you execute the initial stroke, you will switch to your right hand leading with the return stroke. Align your breathing with the stroke. Inhale as you move the stroke toward yourself and exhale as you move the stroke away. * *Because massage moves toxins in the body, it is important to be working toward the heart. This moves the toxins out of the limbs so they may be removed by the blood and lymph systems. Make sure to tell the patient to drink a lot of water for 24 hours to help flush their system.*

With the patient lying supine (face up) on a table, put a pillow or bolster under the knees to keep pressure off the lower back. Start at the head. Gently use your finger tips to massage the scalp in a circular motion. Work towards the forehead continuing the light swirls. Continue to the sides of the face, cheeks, around the lips, and then to the chin. From the chin move up to the ears using you finger tips and thumbs to rub the ears. This is very relaxing. Move to the side of the patient and take their hand. Use a gentle squeezing on the fingers starting at the tips and working toward the palm. Put a small amount of lotion or oil in your hand and warm it. Start at the wrist and use the gliding stroke to work up the arm toward the shoulder. Use light pressure as you move toward the shoulder and no pressure as you return to the wrist. Continue working the entire arm for 3 or 4 cycles.

Repeat using the other arm. Move to the foot of the table. Work the toes with gentle squeezing similar to the way you worked the fingers. Apply more lotion to your hands and warm it. Using the "gliding stroke", begin at the top of the foot and work toward the knee. Avoid going over the knee directly because it can be displaced. Work each side of the shin and sides of the lower leg. Move to the upper leg and thigh and bring the return stroke all the way back to the foot. Repeat using the other leg.

Have the person turn over to the prone (face down) position. Put the pillow or bolster under the ankles. Start at the ankles and work the calf muscles. *Avoid the back of the knee. This area when touched can cause sexual arousal. Continue up to the hamstrings and sides of quadriceps and hip. Move to the head of the table. Starting at the upper back, use effleurage moving toward the lower back.* Avoid putting pressure directly on the spine. Work entire back in a similar manner as the previous routines. The patient may fall asleep. If so, it is a great compliment to you. As you do this type of massage, make mental notes of areas that felt tight or had a lot of heat. This will be an indication of a spasm or energy block.

Hydrotherapy

Hydrotherapy is an ancient healing art that is safe and painless and requires nothing more than the water in your bathroom faucet. The first recorded user of hydrotherapy was Hippocrates in the fourth century B.C. Since then, it has been a part of the healing tradition of every culture. Modern hydrotherapy originated in nineteenth century Austria with the work of Vincent Priessnitz. Water that is slightly cooler than normal body temperature is used to treat insomnia, emotional agitation and menopausal hot flashes. Soak for 20 minutes, adding water as needed to maintain temperature.

Hydrotherapy101. Drinking enough fresh, pure water is essential to our health and well-being. Though caffeinated and alcoholic beverages do contain water, both cause the body to excrete more water than it actually takes in. The result is a fluid deficit, which, over time, can lead to a variety of health problems. These problems become more common in late adulthood, because our need for water actually increases with age. As we age, our mucous membranes become thinner and loose more water. Our kidneys function less efficiently. Water is also valuable as a digestive aid, especially when combined with activated charcoal. (Not the same charcoal used on the backyard grill).

Hydrotherapy treatments require no special equipment. However, specifics such as water temperature and length of application can vary depending on the condition being treated.

Hot baths are used to ease joint pain, constipation, and respiratory ailments. Cold baths relieve fevers and combat fatigue, and herbal baths are popular for relaxation and skin care.

Contrasting Baths, using separate basins of hot and cold water, improve circulation in the pelvic area, speed the healing of urinary tract infection, reduce pelvis pain, and treats ovarian cysts.

Foot Baths aren't just for aching feet. Alternating hot and cold soaks is good for relieving swelling in the feet and legs. By diverting blood away from the affected areas, hot baths are used to relieve head and chest congestion.

Cold Mitten Friction Rubs, in which the skin is rubbed vigorously with a towel or mitten dipped in cold water, are used to increase circulation and fortify the immune system.

Steam Inhalation is used for respiratory conditions such as bronchitis and pneumonia, easing breathing by loosening mucus in the chest. Inhale steam from a pot filled with boiling water.

Hot Compresses applied to the chest are also helpful for respiratory problems.

Cold Compresses can relieve the pain of gout and minimize swelling from bruises and sprains.

Alternating hot and cold Compresses stimulates circulation to help heal sprains and joint   and muscle injuries.

Juice Therapy

Juice therapy is at least 5,000 years old. Juices are a safe and inexpensive form of preventative medicine. Juices provide optimal nutrition yet take little energy to digest. Because you are not spending six hours trying to digest a fatty, high-protein meal, the body has more time and energy to devote to healing itself.

Juice fasting enhances the body's natural healing capacity. The juice fast also helps identify food sensitivities, a major factor in immune system disorders such as arthritis, asthma, and chronic fatigue syndrome. By gradually re-introducing foods after the fast, many people discover that their symptoms worsen when they eat certain foods. Removing the allergen from the diet lifts a tremendous burden from the immune system, so it can fight disease more effectively. A cleansing diet can also be helpful in treating chronic degenerative conditions such as heart disease and arthritis.

Warning: *A hidden medical condition such as diabetes or hypoglycemia can make fasting dangerous without medical supervision.*

One of the reasons that juice fasting is effective is because of substances known collectively as nutrients. These substances include pigments, which give plants their color, and enzymes, substances produced in the plant that help humans digest it. Probably the best known pigments are the carotenes. Though scientists have identified more than 400 different carotenes, the one most people have heard about is beta-carotene, a substance that the body easily converts to vitamin A. Studies show that beta-carotene has potent anti-cancer properties and may actually reverse precancerous conditions such as oral leukoplakia, a pattern of abnormal cell growth that often leads to mouth cancer in people who chew tobacco. A second group of pigments with potential healing power is the flavinoid. Flavinoids give fruits and flowers their vibrant hues. A raw-foods diet featuring plenty of fresh juices is safe for virtually everyone.

Imagery

Imagery is the most fundamental healing technique we have. Everything you do the mind processes through images. Images are not necessarily visual. They can be sounds, tastes, smells, or a combination of sensations. Imagery is the language the mind uses to communicate with the body. It is the biological connection between mind and body.

About 300 years ago, modern Western medicine discarded imagery as a healing tool. This was largely due to the influence of Rene Descartes, a seventeenth-century French philosopher who believed the mind and body were separate and couldn't possibly have any influence on each other.

Unfortunately, many of the images popping into our head do more harm than good. Worry, for example, is very dangerous. The average person has about 10,000 thoughts or images running through their mind each day. At least half of those thoughts are negative. Negative images lead to negative physiology and health. Positive directed images can help your body heal itself.

How imagery works is still largely a mystery. Some evidence suggests that the brain will react the same way to an imagined sensation as to a real one. Imagery is like reality in the sense that if you look at activity in the brain when you're imagining something, it is strikingly similar to the activity that occurs when you're perceiving reality in the limbic system, the part of the brain that deals with the emotions pleasure, pain, fright, and anger. As these images arise in the limbic system, they are interpreted by the cerebral cortex, which is involved in higher brain functions such as reasoning and memory. Without the cerebral cortex, these images would probably be meaningless to us. The limbic system is also connected by the nerves to the hypothalamus, which regulates body temperature, heart rate, hunger, thirst, sleeping, and sexual arousal, and to the pituitary gland, which oversees all of our hormones. After an image forms in the limbic system and is deciphered by the cerebral cortex, the hypothalamus and pituitary gland move into action, casing reactions throughout the body.

If you can learn to use the images in your mind instead of letting them flow over you unchecked, they can have a positive, long-term effect on your health and well-being. It is difficult to master. However, it is just a matter of practice. It's a question of patience and persistence. To improve the quality of your images, become a keen observer of life. Improving your observational skills is the most important thing you can do to make your images more vivid. The best images are the ones that you can conjure for yourself, because they have personal meaning and will help you learn more about yourself than any imagery that is suggested. So, for better or worse, nearly every image has an effect on your body.

Posture Analysis

The muscles in the body can be thought of as rubber bands that allow the bones to work through their range of motion. For example, the biceps flex to curl the arm up, while the triceps that are opposite the biceps extend the arm out straight. The erector spinae muscles that extend along the spine are balanced by the abdominal muscles. This balancing of muscle tension can be observed through posture analysis. Excess tension in a certain muscle group will cause the body to deviate from an erect and level position.

To perform a posture analysis, ask the patient to face away from you and close their eyes. Have them take a deep breath and relax. Look at their shoulders. Does one shoulder appear lower than the other? Now look at their hips. Is one raised above the other? Draw a stick figure on a sheet of paper. Note these differences by drawing a line that shows any abnormality in the shoulders. Now draw a line that shows any abnormality in the hips. Ask the patient to turn to the side. Look at their back. Is it curved more in the lower region? Is their upper back hunched over? Using a stick figure again, note any of these abnormalities. This analysis will give you an idea of which muscles may be tight and pulling more than is necessary to maintain an erect posture. Practice this posture analysis as you watch people throughout the day. It will make planning a strategy for a massage much easier.

Endangerment Sites

There are areas of the body that should be avoided because the underlying structures can cause damage to blood vessels and nerves if pressure is applied. These are called "endangerment sites" These areas should be learned before you begin to use any firm pressure in your massage.

1. The *anterior (front) triangle of the neck* which is bordered by the Sternocleidomastoid (SCM) muscle, trachea and jaw. The carotid artery, jugular vein and vague nerve are in this area.
2. The *posterior (rear) triangle of the neck* which is bordered by the SCM, trapezius muscle and the clavicle. The brachial plexus, subclavian artery and external jugular vein are located here.
3. The *arm pit*. There are several nerves, arteries and lymph nerves located here.
4. The *anterior bend of the elbow*. The radial and ulnar arteries are found here.
5. The *funny bone*. The ulnar nerve is located here.
6. The *femoral triangle* which is found in the crease of the hip and lower abdomen. The femoral veins and artery are located here along with lymph nodes.
7. The *posterior aspect of the knee*. This is called the popliteal area. The popliteal artery and vein are located in this area.
8. The *upper area of the abdomen* below the ribs. There are many organs accessible here.
9. The *lower back* below the ribs. The kidneys are located here.

Massage techniques at the Water Healing level become more therapeutic. These techniques will be added to the relaxation sequence that was learned in Earth Belt. The techniques emphasize concentrating on locating and treating muscle spasms and energy blockages. The pressure used will be slightly firmer than that of the relaxation massage.

The stroke that is used for working the muscles to loosen tension is called Petrissage. This is performed by using a kneading type movement of the hands. The hands pull the fibers of the muscles in a swirling motion. The hands are overlapped, as one pulls the muscle, the other reaches over to perform the same motion. They are circled toward each other which will move and stretch the fibers of muscle. This stroke is used after the muscle has been warmed with effleurage. To effectively use this stroke, stand to the side of the limb being worked and perform petrissage toward the heart. Use the gliding stroke to return to where you started and begin the kneading again. Perform a few extra times over areas of tension. This stroke will primarily be used on the extremities and back. Have the patient drink lots of water for 24 hours after the session to flush toxins out of their body.

Approximately half the cause for death in the United States is linked to the food we eat. Up until the early 20th century, food therapy was widely practiced as a way of healing the sick and keeping the healthy well. Before that, we were primarily a nation of small farmers. People ate the nutritional food they grew. Their gardens served as their medicine chest and their kitchens a pharmacy. During the industrial revolution, there came a new way of eating, and new attitude toward food. In 1905, Henry Ford began to impact the American eating habits and diet. The American diet went from low-fat, high-fiber and plant based to one that is centered on high-fat, low-fiber animal sources. People rarely got cancer or heart attacks before the 20th century. The first recorded heart attack in America was in 1908 in the journal of the American Medical Association.

By the end of WWII we started relying on the "wonder" drug penicillin which was developed during that war. Foods went from being whole and nutritious to being processed and refined and void of necessary nutrients. The 1960's ushered in the era of the "fast-food" restaurant and the rest of our nutritional health is history. Many Americans were raised with the mistaken notion that protein makes us big and strong, so we ate huge amounts of meat and drank large amounts of milk. This has led to a dramatic increase in cancer, arthritis, and other health problems. Reduce fat and increase fiber. This will lower the risk of developing certain diseases and help the body's ability to recover from them. Phyto-chemicals, which are natural chemicals found in all plants, but not in most vitamin supplements, protects the plant against stress, disease, and being eaten by animals. Our bodies need oxygen to stay alive, but too much of it causes severe damage to cells. Cigarette smoke, car exhaust, and oxidizing chlorine lead to oxidation. Oxidation leads to premature aging and weakens immunity. Wrinkles, cataracts, arthritis, cancer, and heart disease are strongly linked to oxidation. That's right! We are rusting!

When most people talk about antioxidants, they are usually referring to vitamins C and E, beta-carotene and selenium. However, other food qualities, such as phyto-chemicals and carotenoids also contain antioxidants. It may be easier to take vitamins. But if you are really concerned about your health, there is only one thing to do. Eat right! (Oh yeah, and get plenty of exercise and sleep).

In the past almost all medicines were herbs. Aspirin's main ingredient is acetylsalicylic acid, which is isolated from the bark of a willow tree. Herbs do not work quickly for chronic health problems. The main reason people do not notice a result in herbal therapies is that they give up too soon. Since herbal remedies are not standardized, it is important to experiment with what the therapeutic dose is for you. Always err on the side of caution.

Ways to Ingest Herbs

Tea is the most common.

Capsule/Tablets. Swallowing tablets is probably the easiest way to take any medicine.

Extracts/Tinctures. Technically, extracts are stronger and more concentrated than tinctures. However, today, these terms are generally used interchangeably.

Ointments/Creams. Herbs can be mixed with massage oils and creams. Almond oil is a common base.

Herbs used in Healing

Chamomile, in tea form is a gentle relaxant. It has antispasmodic, anti-infective, and anti-inflammatory uses.

Garlic can lower blood pressure, blood cholesterol levels, fights against tumors, aids digestion, and relieves gas.

Ginkgo is particularly useful for treating problems caused by decreased blood flow to the brain. Elderly people who suffer from memory loss caused by circulation problems will often find that mental clarity increases when they take ginkgo. Ginkgo can prevent blood clots and mood swings, relieve symptoms of tinnitus, asthma, phlebitis, and vertigo.

Milk Thistles are used to treat liver conditions, including hepatitis and cirrhosis. It contains a flavinoid called Silymarin that works directly on liver cells.

Saint-John's-Wort is traditionally used as a muscle relaxant and as a mild tranquilizer. The active compound functions as an MAO inhibitor.

Valerian is a safe, effective alternative to prescription sleeping pills and tranquilizers.

Reflexology

As long as humans have been walking they have been rubbing their feet. But it wasn't until the early twentieth century that modern reflexology began to develop (often credited to William Fitzgerald, M.D.) Eunice Ingham, an American massage therapist, using Fitzgerald's work, developed special massage techniques and created "maps" of the feet that showed which spots to touch to aid healing elsewhere in the body.

Reflexologists believe that certain spots on your foot are directly linked to other parts of the body, including muscles, bones, and organs. Working these spots help the body to relax, returns the natural balance and also gives it a chance to heal. The concept is that pressure applied to the feet (and hands) promotes a beneficial response throughout the body, providing a break from stress. Relaxation is the key. Stress and tension are responsible for about 75% of all health problems. Reducing stress helps everything function better. Reflexologists believe the body is divided into ten "energy zones" that run from your head to your toes. The foot contains more than 7,000 nerves. Reducing stress allows the body to return to its natural state of balance, called homeostasis.

Reflexology works best when it is used for prevention. It helps keep your body running smoothly by improving circulation, cleaning your impurities, balancing your system, and giving you more energy. This is why it is a good idea to make reflexology part of your daily routine instead of waiting for problems to occur.

Vitamins and Minerals

Nearly half of all Americans use supplements at least occasionally. Supplements can benefit a person's health because they contain much higher doses of key nutrients than you find in foods. Supplements are generally safe, especially if they are not grossly abused.

Vitamins were discovered around 1906 (probably related to Henry Ford somehow). What triggered the search for vitamins was the fact that fat, protein, and carbohydrates were found to be insufficient to sustain life. In 1912, the term vitamin was coined (for "vital amine"). Vitamin supplements were on the public market by 1925. Vitamins were named alphabetically in the order they were discovered. There are at least 13 vitamins and 15 minerals essential for good health. Vitamins are organic compounds, they contain carbon. Minerals are simpler, non-organic compounds and are usually found in foods in smaller amounts. Vitamins and minerals, along with fatty acids and amino acids are among the 50 known essential nutrients for a healthy life. Four vitamins are fat-soluble (A, D, E, and K), meaning that excess amounts may be stored in the body. The others (C and the eight B vitamins) are water-soluble, so excess amounts are urinated away.

Minerals are classified in two categories. The first are the major minerals, or macronutrients, such as calcium, magnesium, and potassium, which are found in relatively high concentrations in food. The second group, are the trace minerals, or micronutrients, such as chromium, copper, iron, and zinc. These are usually found in only minute amounts. Every cell in your body needs every vitamin, but not every cell utilizes them the same way or needs the same amount.

Aromatherapy

The term aromatherapy was coined in the late 1920's, although aromatic plants have played a role in maintaining health for thousands of years. Ancient civilizations used oils for massage, bathing, medicine, burning incense in religious ceremonies, and to embalm the dead. The development of synthetic drugs in the late 1800s began the decline of traditional healing with aromatics. Rene-Maurice Gasttefosse revived it in the late 1920's. Aromatherapy did not become popularly used in the United States until the 1980's.

Essential oils work on the body on several different levels. The most obvious is by stimulating the sense of smell. Smells act directly on the brain. It is the only sense that is hard wired to the brain. A life without fragrance seems to lead to a high incidence of psychiatric problems such as anxiety and depression. While most depressed, stressed out people can smell, their emotional states affect the odors. Lavender increases alpha waves in the back of the head. Jasmine increases beta waves in the front of the head.

Experiencing the mood-altering power of scent can be as simple as adding several drops of essential oil to your bath or on a warm light bulb. A longer-lasting way to scent a room is with an aroma lamp or electric diffuser. Essential oils are also effective when used topically. Unlike mineral oils, which just hang around on the skin, essential oils are made up of very small molecules that actually penetrate through the skin into the blood system. Another topical use of essential oils is aromatherapy massage. Light can damage essential oils. Therefore, use tinted glass bottles and store them in a cool dark place.

Essential Oils for Beginners

Citrus oils are great for relieving a somber mood.

Floral oils are used to relieve stress.

Lavender soothes cuts, bruises, and insect bites.

Peppermint is a great mental stimulant. Apply under the nose and behind the ears. Peppermint can also ease intestinal discomfort.

Rosemary is a stimulant.

Tea Tree is the best all around natural antiseptic available. It kills 99.9% of all bacteria. It is the fastest penetrating oil and can be used to stop infection and to speed healing of cuts, wounds or any infection.

Sound Therapy

What you hear can help or hurt your health. About 2,500 years ago, the Greek mathematician and philosopher Pythagoras developed "Prescriptions" of music for his students. (Not to be confused with the Pythagorean Theorem). He told them which sounds would help them work, relax, sleep, and wake up better.

Ancient societies used tones in rituals to open metaphysical doorways, just the same as in "Close Encounters of the Third Kind". The qualities of sound are velocity, frequency, and intensity. High-tech devices such as the ultrasound machines help heal soft-tissue injuries and to make diagnostic photographs of fetuses in their mother's womb. The heart will automatically attempt to adjust its beat to match the rhythm of the sound. Sounds can also affect your breathing, blood pressure, and muscle tension, and cause the release of endorphins. Science has long known that every atom vibrates, emitting sound waves even though they are too faint to hear. Since body parts are made up of atoms, they all produce sound waves. These sound waves are altered when disease or stress sets in. Directing healing sound waves at the body can restore natural rhythms and encourage and support healing. This technique is called cymatic therapy.

Another theory holds that sound waves can balance energy centers, or chakras. When there are disruptions to the chakras caused by stress, disease, and other factors, the frequencies are thrown off. By applying specific sounds to the body, the chakras can be returned to normal, and the body will heal itself. Sound is a good healer, but noise isn't. Noise is a hazard. Even if it doesn't hurt your ears, the rest of you may be. Noise pollution is linked to high blood pressure, stress, lack of concentration, and irritability. Excessive noise increases your risk of high blood pressure and other cardiovascular problems by as much as 10 percent. Women are often at greater risk than men. That's because they can hear higher frequencies. Tools of sound therapy can include musical instruments, tapes, tuning forks, machines, and voice.

Hum Therapy

A simple form of sound therapy is "Hum" therapy. It's cheap, no complex tools or techniques. You probably don't need much practice and you don't need a physician.

The sounds you make with your own voice can be the most powerful healer of all. Toning is a process, which involves making elongated vowel sounds. The vibrations from the tones can help relax you, ease stress, and balance the mind and body.

Key Largo is relaxing music. Slow tempos are largo. This can reduce your heart and breathing rate, calm your body, and help it heal itself. This music should be at 60 beats per minute or less. Natural sounds such as rustling leaves, running water, wind whipping through the trees, or the rain are also relaxing.

Yoga

Yoga is the most basic of natural remedies. You don't need anything but quiet. The term yoga comes from the Sanskrit word yuj, meaning to "yoke". The purpose of yoga is to yoke - to join or balance - the mind, body, and breath. When the mind is disturbed, the breath and body are affected. The earliest mention of Yoga comes from small stone symbols in India that are thought to date from 3000 B.C. About 2,300 years ago, the sage Patanjali compiled this passed-down knowledge in the Yoga Sutras, which include the eight steps that lead to spiritual enlightenment. Breathing techniques are called pranayama. Other steps include moral codes such as a dedication to nonviolence and severe simplicity.

Yoga heals in two ways. The first is through relaxation. The second is through "squeezing". Moving your body into different poses will force blood out of vital organs, allowing fresh blood to take its place. This gives your organs more nutrients, making them stronger and resistant to disease. When you practice pranayama, you change your normal patterns of breathing, which in turn calms your state of mind, reducing the disturbances and impurities in your body. Daily yoga routines come in four parts: breathing, relaxation, meditation, and poses. Your routine should last at least a half-hour and should begin with breathing.

Deep breathing draws energy into your body and provides you with precious oxygen and calms your muscles and organs. The proper way to breath is by using the diaphragm. When the diaphragm flexes, it pulls down and opens the lower lobes of your lungs, allowing more air inside. Yoga offers many different advanced breathing techniques. The best overall stress reducer is called the complete breath.

There are dozens and dozens of poses, with little change over the centuries. Some stretches strengthen muscle others improve posture and skeletal system. Some compress and relax organs and nerves. Always wind down and relax, ending with the corpse pose and five to ten minutes of relaxation exercises. Inhale energy and healing, exhale fatigue and stress, or whatever is adversely affecting your well-being. Here are some benefits of common yoga poses.

Benefits of Yoga Poses

1. The Mountain pose. An easy standing pose, that helps with osteoporosis.
2. Standing sun pose. Helps with constipation and bladder problems, loosens hips and shoulders, and improves nerve function.
3. Tree pose. A standing pose that tones our legs and improves balance, concentration, and breathing.
4. The Dancer pose. Improves balance, opens nasal passages, strengthens hips and thighs, and helps relieve fatigue.
5. Windmill pose. Loosens hips and lower back, and improves breathing.
6. The Corpse pose. Helps prevent back pain, stress and high blood pressure.
7. Knee squeeze. Relieves gas, increases circulation in your head and neck, eases lower back pain, and strengthens stomach muscles.

8. Spine twist. Helps prevent constipation and bladder problems.
9. Head-to-knee. Helps improve the function of internal organs.
10. The Seated Sun pose. Helps aid digestion and impotence.
11. Baby pose. Limbers your lower back, improves digestion, and relieves stiffness.
12. The Easy Bridge pose. Helps with back pain and fatigue, improves circulation to your head and face, improves your endocrine system and reduces blood pressure.
13. The Boat pose. Aids digestion and helps vital organs function more efficiently.
14. Half Boat pose. Use to work up to the full boat pose.
15. The Cobra pose. Strengthens the entire body, aids digestion, makes your spine more flexible and improves eyesight.
16. Lion pose. Relaxes facial muscles and ease tension.

Healing with Chi

The techniques for Wind Healing deal with subtle energy healing. Focused intention is used to guide chi in order to assist healing. Having an attitude of wanting to heal the person is necessary for the techniques to be effective. You should be studying meridian charts and learning the direction of chi flow in the body.

These methods are based on my personal experience and are a mixture of acupressure, Jin Shin modalities, Polarity Therapy, and Therapeutic Touch. These techniques can be performed with the patient fully clothed. This makes them appropriate for "on the spot" healing. I have used these methods on my students during class to relieve pain, energy blocks and spasms.

Each of your hand has a polarity to them. In most people, the right hand is Yang. It sends energy out. The left hand is Yin which receives energy. In order to find out which hand is Yin or Yang the following exercise can be practiced. You will need 2 people: Both of you should warm your hands by rubbing them together. Have the other person hold up one of their hands with the palm cupped and relaxed. Pass your right hand in front of their hand. Ask them if they feel warmth. Now pass your left hand in front of their hand. Ask them if it feels cooler than the right. Repeat if necessary. If your right hand is warmer then your left, then your polarity is Right hand/Yang, Left hand/Yin, (which is the polarity of most people.) This means you will use your right hand to send energy into the patient and your left hand at the drainage points. The "local point" is the area or point of irritation or pain. With the back of your hand, palpate for heat or thickness to the area. You may find a sensitive spot or even a spasm that is difficult to release. With your right hand palm or finger tips, press into this point. Try to feel the pulsing of energy in the point. This will take some practice, but after a while you will feel the pulsing easily. The "distal point" or point for release will usually be found at the insertion end of a muscle, or further along the same meridian that the local point is found. You should in a sense "feel" into the local point and "listen" to its direction. Allow your intuitive feelings to move your left hand.

You will know that you have found the distal point when another feeling of warmth can be felt with the left hand. With your left hand on the distal point breathe energy into the local point. Exhale and imagine energy coming out of your right hand and into the muscle or meridian, traveling along it to your left hand. As you inhale, draw the energy out with your left hand. Keep your knees slightly bent so the excess energy will be grounded out into the ground. Sometimes a popping will be felt when an energy block or spasm is released. Feel the pulses coming from the local and distal points. When they have synchronized with each other the meridian is cleared.

Energy drainage points

If you are having trouble finding the distal points here are a few general areas that will work until your ability to palpate has improved.

1. The area between C7 and T1 vertebrae is a distal drain point for all Yang meridians. I use this point when working on the back.

2. There are drainage points on the lateral aspect of both shoulders, between the anterior and posterior deltoids. Used for upper trapezius.

3. At the wrist we have Heart 5 and Lung 8. These drainage points are used for arm releases. You can grab around the persons wrist and you will be right on these. They drain chi from the arms.

4. The medial aspect of the leg at the knee can be used when working on the quadriceps.

5. The medial malleolus (inside of the ankle) can be used for a distal point in the lower extremities.

GV and CV clearing

This sequence is used for self healing. It clears blockages in the Governing and Conceptual vessels. The flow of energy within these vessels gives the body energy. Clearing them is like a tune-up to the whole body. They balance appetite, clears the eyes, head, throat, chest, digestive organs, pelvis, as well as lymph, blood and nervous system.

Using both of your hands, begin by holding the top of your head with the fingers of your right hand while holding the third eye with the fingers of the left hand. Hold both points until you feel a pulsing sensation in your fingers, then move the left fingers to the point below the nose and above the upper lip, feeling for the pulse again. Leave your right hand on top of your head while you move your left hand to the V of the throat, then the center of the chest, base of the sternum, navel, and then pubis.

Move your right hand from the top of your head to your coccyx. Reach behind with your left hand and place on your spine at the ming men (point opposite the dan tien; literally 'the great energy source') while keeping your right hand at the coccyx, all the while feeling for the pulsing. Reach your left hand over the shoulders to the point between the shoulder blades, then to the jade gate (occiput), then the left hand moves to the top of your head. *This will assist you in opening the Microcosmic orbit and should be performed regularly.

Chapter 4

Hoshin Tao Chi Kung

Chi or subtle energy is an area of research that has grown in acceptance in Western culture and medicine. Science is just now beginning to measure and test its existence. Once thought of as the "legends" of ancient masters, Chi Kung or breath work (meditation) methods are being used to treat illness, depression, anxiety and an array of other mental and physical problems.

Chi is recognized cross culturally as a basic component in all things. Different animals, people and plants give off a varying amount of this energy. Inanimate objects also have an energy essence to them. The difference is in energy type (Yin or Yang) and vibrational frequency. Rocks give off a slower vibration than plants, which are on a slower frequency than animals. Inanimate objects can be charged with chi using intention. The use of focused intention can be seen in shamanism, Wicca, faith healers, reiki practitioners and esoteric healers of all type. Chi is a neutral force. The intentions of the person make it good or bad. This can be seen in both the inward and outward process of chi development.

In Hoshin Tao Chi Kung, the most important exercise is called the secret smile. This exercise is used to fill your mind and body with positive intention. If you try to move energy while angry you will tend to get a burning sensation from the Yang (hot masculine energy) along with fun things like migraines, sore muscles and insomnia. The same is true with internal journeying. You must have a positive attitude as you go into yourself. As your energy levels grow and your chakras (energy centers along the spine) begin to open, you will be presented with the positive and negative aspects of yourself. Both must be understood and accepted in order to evolve up the spiritual ladder and move on to the next level of learning.

The secret smile fills you with happy intention. When the darker thoughts and emotions surface, you will have a much easier time not getting depressed or caught in a negative thinking pattern. The dark side of ourselves must be accepted in order to have a balanced view of what motivates us. Why aren't you what you see as negative? A 'crack head' is not something most aspire to be. Our socially learned self (sometimes called ego) drives us to not be what we see as bad. However, anyone if put in the perfect set of circumstances could do things they would never want to take credit for. I cannot stress enough how important it is to focus on positive thinking. I have seen and experienced firsthand what clinical paranoia can do to someone. It is a negative side effect of inner work that can be avoided to the greater extent. Smiling is a powerful thing. Intention is seen in the face of everyone you talk to each day. Try to notice the expressions on people's faces. Do they seem happy? If you give a simple smile to a stranger who seems to be having a less than good day, you can change his entire mindset. Energy is subtle, yet its influence is extremely powerful. The grumpy person may see you smile and feel a bit better, going about the rest of their day being a little kinder than they would have. This is an example of how energy is transmitted through intention. The reverse is true also. Putting good feelings into the world sure can't be a bad thing. Think about it.

Path Notes of an American Ninja Master by Dr. Glenn J. Morris contains the basic Hoshin Tao Chi Kung exercises. *Path Notes* is the guide for the aspiring Hoshin practitioner. It is the first book that a new Hoshin student reads. All of the exercises were developed by Dr. Morris based on self experimentation with Chinese Chi Kung and the Hindu chakra system. The techniques follow a set of exercises that systematically prepare the body and mind for chi development. This training is the core of Hoshin and is what sets Hoshin Jutaijutsu apart from other modern martial arts systems. Development of chi is the primary goal of Hoshin.

First the mind is calmed through one pointed focus. Next a positive attitude is developed along with methods for collecting and storing chi. If followed correctly, one should start to see results within 90 days. At first one will get the breathing techniques which make the body relax and align for longer meditation periods. The phosphenes behind the eyes are watched as a diagnostic device. The color of each particular chakra will begin to appear in the smoky black that is usually seen when you close your eyes. It will look like smoke with light behind it.

Each chakra has a particular attitude and frequency. If you start to see a red tint to the phosphenes then your earth chakra is dominant. With each color you are seeing a reflection of chakra energy. As your practice continues, you will begin to see fractal like patterns within the colors you are getting. These fractals may begin to change into geometric shapes. Sometimes sacred geometry will appear. As more chi is developed through storing in the hara (dan tien), the geometric patterns begin to look like landscapes. These landscapes will begin to get more detailed. As you visit these areas, make note of what any inhabitants look like. What is around you?

These areas in the void are images of a certain energy or chakra realm. There are three areas or dimensions if you will. In the beginning your focus will be looking downward into the body. This allows the physical body to be probed for any areas that may be weak or blocked. Once the body is given attention your eyes will look straight forward. By looking forward you will see into the local area. Spirits who exist close to the physical plane will be attracted to you. They may appear in your inner vision as lights that float around in front of your face. Usually it is a good idea to just ignore them as they can be a distraction to higher states. When you look up you are sending energy to the 3rd eye. This will increase the detail that is seen in an elemental realm. When you have developed a high level of chi and can project into the void, this eye focus will send you into the lower, middle and upper realms. These are described in shamanism and other esoteric traditions for spirit communication. When I experimented with these eye gazes it had a profound effect. I once looked down into my body and then down into the ground. I began to fly downward. I could see that I was in a rectangular stone tunnel. I felt like I was moving 100 mph. As I flew down this tunnel, I could see in the distance a light that looked like a fire reflecting down a hallway. I could feel that it was getting warmer as the exit to the tunnel got closer. I had an uneasy feeling creep over me. I knew I probably wasn't supposed to be there, but my curiosity kept me moving forward. I could see the exit, like a fire lit doorway coming at me. Then the movement slowed and I was floating just in front of the exit. I saw what looked like an underground cavern. There was a grim feeling of unease about it. I stuck my head out of the exit and when I looked to my left, I saw a figure that looked like Damo (Boddhidarma). He was wearing rags and his face looked wrinkled and grey. I excused myself and thought of my body, which is all that is needed to bring you out of a scary meditation.

I was back in myself and sweating profusely. I called Glenn the next morning and he informed me that it was Damo and that he had been made a gate keeper for the underworld. Glenn used to joke that hell is not all bad. According to Glenn, Damo was the sage who brought esoteric yoga and Chi Kung concepts to the Chinese. He was imprisoned under a rock in hell for not admitting he had lied about being a descendant of a Chinese fairy. He was given the chance to retract the lie he told his whole life and he refused. Doc had asked that he be released so he could speak with him.

When I gazed forward I would see images of people from different historical periods. They usually popped in looking curiously at me like; "Who is this?" then floated off. Glenn always told me to ignore the local fauna. He said the ones worth questioning are the shape shifters. They are the true immortals. They are found in the upper realms. Just before the Kundalini peak happened, without any effort on my part, my eyes would roll up and I would be looking into the top of my head. I would get the angelic archetypes who give empathic feelings of comfort and universal acceptance.

The tongue works as a switch to the appropriate chakra centers. When first starting out, the tongue is placed just behind the upper front teeth where they insert into the gums. This will center and relax the body. As you gain energy and begin moving up the chakras, the tongue will change position. It moves from behind the teeth towards the soft palate in the back of the roof of the mouth. If trouble with insomnia is experienced you can drop the tongue to the gums at the bottom front teeth. This disconnects the 2 main meridians that make the small orbit. Once the small orbit or Lesser Kan and Li is opened, the larger orbits including the arms and legs called Greater Kan and Li are practiced.

As you develop your internal wattage, strange things will begin to happen. The more you meditate and store energy, the faster effects will manifest. If you are practicing the Damo's cave meditation, your cave and the inhabitants will change. The siddhis (extraordinary abilities) Glenn described are just symptoms that remind you there is more work to be done. Keep going. Keep your tongue up. Stay positive and have no fear. The end results are well worth the time invested in practice.

Chi development can dramatically increase athletic ability, especially in a dangerous situation. In the summer of

2007, my top student Chris Robinson was enjoying a family outing at the beach at Oregon Inlet, near Nags Head, N.C. His 12 year old niece was paddling around in one of the kayaks they had brought with them. The tide was strong and the current from the inlet began carrying her out to sea. Once her family looked up to see where she was, she was very far out in the ocean. She was carried about a mile offshore, past a group of fishing boats competing in a tournament. The fishermen paid no attention to the kayak. Chris's family began to panic and called the Coast Guard. The Coast Guard informed them that they had an emergency that they were in route to and it would be at least 45 minutes until they could respond. His 16 year old nephew decided to try and paddle out to help his sister. He became fatigued and was unable to paddle back, drifting out to where his sister was.

Fearing the worst, Chris assessed the situation and decided that he was going to go after them. His family was in a panic around him, their voices filled with fear and desperation. He looked out into the water and realized there was a chance he would not make it back. He began deep belly breathing and went into mushin (no mind). The voices around him faded and he was focused on the mission he faced. He strapped a boogie board to his ankle, ran up the beach a few blocks to get the proper trajectory to intercept the kids and dove into the cold water. A wave crashed into him as he was coming up and he swallowed a mouthful of salt water. He puked up the water and felt a tremendous amount of energy come up inside him. His mind went blank and he again began swimming out to the now tiny spec that was the helpless children.

As he would begin to tire using one swimming stroke, he would switch to another. He continued to alternate strokes as he went further and further out into the ocean. He lost his boogie board in the rough sea, which he had brought to save his life. He continued swimming toward the kids. Up ahead, he approached the fishing boats and it suddenly dawned on him that there were probably sharks in the area. He swam right through the boats to the area were the kayaks had slowed down. After swimming for an hour, he finally reached the kayaks. The two were holding on to each other's kayak. His niece was hysterical. He settled her down, had the boy jump in the kayak with his sister, and emptied the other kayak. They traded kayaks and he emptied the 2nd one. He tied the 2 kayaks together and began paddling them back to shore with his nephew in the kayak with him and his niece on the bow, towing the other kayak.

He was surprised to find that paddling back was much harder than swimming out with the combined weight of all of them, the 2 kayaks, on top of the strong current. He made it back to his frantic relatives who hugged him and cried tears of joy at their safe return. Chris is the only person I know who could have done this. At 41, he has the best physical fitness of anyone I know. He is a professional volleyball player, extreme mountain biker, rock climber, scuba diver and all around manic.

I once called him during a severe tropical storm and he was jogging in the woods. He yelled "Whoa!" then again, "Shit!" I asked him what was happening and he said he was seeing poisonous snakes all over the trail. The snakes were escaping the rising water around the rivers and the park was temporarily closed due to the snake warning. He was jumping over and dodging them like it was fun, and scary. Chris was the uke for Doc and me as we revised the Hoshinjutsu curriculum. I trained him from White Belt to his current rank of 7th Dan. His first question ever to me was "Can you demonstrate chi for me?" I showed him the polarity in each of his hands and what Yin and Yang energies feel like. He had been a high school biology teacher and was used to examining things from a scientific viewpoint. He felt the differences in energy types, looked at me and said "Ok." He is a living testimony to what focused intention and chi can accomplish.

Chapter 5

Kundalini Awakening

Kundalini is a dormant energy that lies at the base of the spine. When it rises, it effects the chakra, endocrine and physiological systems in the body. The effects of Kundalini awakening are permanent. This is the real difference between Kundalini and other spiritual emergences/emergencies. Near Death Experiences, astral travel, and the development of chi all give similar effects, but the Kundalini is much stronger and does not subside. Those who have done it know each other. We can tell. I know very few who have Kundalini, though lots of people I know have developed chi. James Alexander, Santiago Dobles, Tao Semko and Jared Guinn all experienced similar effects from Kundalini awakening. Jared, having had the smoothest process yet, is a sign that the current Kundalini Awakening Process that we are teaching has improved.

Santiago and Tao are incredible individuals who teach Tantra, Yoga, Reiki and holistic healing. They are the founders of UMAA Tantra, which offers training in an array of eso-science. The "boys" as Doc called them worked with Glenn to improve the Hoshin Tao Chi Kung techniques and created a refined method for faster and safer Kundalini awakening. Glenn had released an endorsement on the Improved K.A.P. website just 2 weeks before his death. It was and is his latest research and I am proud that we can continue offering it to the world. Santiago and Tao teach this amazing and updated version of Glenn's methods for achieving a permanent Kundalini awakening.

Those that have Kundalini are living in a similar perceptual reality. We are changed and can tell others who have awakened it. To someone who doesn't have it awakened, they can tell by looking at the Kundalini survivor's aura, which tends to be thick around the head and mostly misty white. The awakened individual feels electrical in close proximity, like static electricity on a piece of cloth. The eyes seem to be on fire, with a glowing ring around the iris. The natural energy type is enhanced. Yin folks feel cold and have a slow pulsing vibration. Yang dominant Kundalini survivors feel like a fast, strong static. The skilled can switch between the two once they figure out how.

Once I made the decision to go for the Kundalini, I was still a bit nervous about how I would be afterward. Would I go nuts? Would I be able to function in society? I thought long and hard before I was ready to commit to making it happen. Glenn told me that not everyone can do it. He said "I think I only got it because I was really stubborn." He didn't know exactly what to expect as he was the original guinea pig for his method. He told me "Being Yin, you will probably have to heat up to get the fireworks. You are lucky. Most folks pop then have to figure out how to cool down. You already have that part."

So I began my practice. I had received Shakti energy transmission from Doc to jump start the awakening. I always started my meditation in the traditional Hoshin Tao Chi Kung way; secret smile, orbits, five point breathing and bone breathing. I used the visualization of balls of fire coming in the crown, hands and feet, mixing with my orbits. After these I would just melt and observe my phosphenes to see what might appear. I began to get a fast vibration in my sacrum that would move up into my lower back. At first I thought this was my muscles shaking from sitting erect, but I would relax totally and it would still be there. My body would do this for upwards of an hour during meditation, yet I was never sore or fatigued from it. Glenn explained that these were kriyas or tremors in the spine caused by Kundalini being stirred and awakened. As the days went on, the vibrations were getting much stronger and felt like I was a candle flame flickering. I would vibrate slowly then it would get very fast. The phosphenes began to make fractals that would turn into geometric shapes and patterns. This continued for a week or so of meditating every day.

One evening, I was sitting, shaking like usual and a face surrounded in flames appeared to me. I could feel the heat of the flames on my face. The face was dark blue with the tongue sticking out. I was looking into the face of Kali, the goddess of death. The heat sensation became uncomfortable and I focused my attention on my body. I opened my eyes and stretched out but the vibration sensation was still present. I usually felt the kriyas during meditation only. Now I could feel that tingling all the time. I continued doing my sitting sessions and with each meditation I was getting intense fractal and geometric patterns which formed sacred geometric shapes and holographs. I could hear a whooshing sound in my ears that was getting so loud I couldn't hear the music over it. My attention was focusing on the vibrations in my body, which the whooshing sound was synchronizing to. This became the only meditation I could perform. I could try any other meditation such as Damo's cave or the mental vacation and I would go right back to the shaking violently and explosions of white behind my eyes.

Finally one night it came to a peak. I felt like my whole body had spasmed and an intense blast of energy came up my back and blasted out of my head. I saw the brightest white light that I have ever seen. It was like a huge explosion inside me. I was caught in this position, body tight and hearing the loud roar in my ears. All I could see was white light. I felt like I was holding my breath so I tried to relax a bit. I looked out into the white and it began to twinkle and dissipate. As I looked out through the white dissolving I could see outer space. Now normally when I saw visions behind my eyes the images would track my head movements. If I turned my head the image remained in front of me. This was different. I could look around out there. I saw constellations and planets. A holographic white tiger appeared in front of me. It looked as though it were walking down an invisible tree branch toward me. I was locked in this state for what felt like only a few minutes. I felt my senses returning as I became aware of my body, which felt like I had worked out for hours. I looked at the clock and I had been meditating for almost 3 hours. I was sweating and had tremors in my whole body. I crawled over to my bed and tried to fall asleep. I could still hear the train sound in my ears. I felt my mind thinking at an accelerated rate. It was not conscious reasoning but a mix of random thoughts bouncing back and forth. Like a computer solving a complicated problem. I dropped my tongue down and began deep breathing. My nerves were fried and I was trembling all over. I opened my eyes when I heard my alarm clock going off.

I never fell asleep. I was just observing this dance of opposite viewpoints in my mind. It was as if all of the viewpoints from the experiences of my life were being examined to fix negative thought patterns they had caused.

I was a guitar teacher at the time. I went to work and set up in my studio. My first student of the day arrived around 9:30am. The lessons were 30 minutes each and the first few were basic music theory, which I could teach in my sleep. Around 11 or so I began to feel my consciousness shift. I looked over to make sure the student was in the right position on the guitar and I saw a pale transparent image of an older man separate away from the young boy's body. I tried to ignore it but it wasn't fading away like most ghost sightings. I finished the lesson and went out to greet the next student, a William and Mary College professor. I was seeing similar apparitions and lights around him. I went for a coffee break, trying to relax and get myself calmed down. Around 2pm I realized that the "visions" had stopped. It seemed to start again around 6pm and last roughly 2 hours. This went on for days. During those times of day and night I felt like the physical world and the spiritual world would overlap. Doc said it probably had something to do with the Yin and Yang cycles of my body. It seemed like I was going nuts. At least I had a job that allowed me to hide it. I could feel energy coming up my spine, out of my head, then raining down and coming back in my hands and feet. This feeling never went away. I still feel it today.

You can't "turn off" Kundalini. It is always there. You have to use it in a creative or productive way to keep the energy from pulling you into paranoia. As the endocrine system kicked in and dumped chemicals into my body, I had radical mood swings. I would think long and hard on the traumatic events of my life. Until I had accepted their effect on me or come to grips with them, the thoughts would stay in the forefront of my mind. I believe that Kundalini can shave negative karma. It is the psychological process of overcoming negativity from this life or another. The Buddhists say that when a person reaches enlightenment they break the wheel of Samsara (death and rebirth). It seems that in order to evolve up the spiritual ladder, you must atone for past mistakes or shortcomings. May just be self analysis, but after Kundalini my life sure went crazy. It was as though I had to experience bad things in order to work out my karma. The internal process relates to your chakra attitudes. Once Kundalini is awakened, your chakras are fully activated and the negative emotions that are hidden deep in our subconscious must be accepted in order to evolve spiritually. Hoshin Tao Chi Kung is a great way to prepare the body and mind for this process.

The new Kundalini Awakening Process training helps work through this evolution. It can be scary if you don't understand why it is happening. Smile. Be happy. Life is good. There are lessons in everything that happens to us. Learn what you need to from the hard times. You will be a better human being for it.

As the siddhis begin to manifest, you will have interesting things happen. Empathy will be one of the first to arise. You may notice you share the thoughts and feelings of the people you surround yourself with. This can be a blessing and a curse. When this began to intensify with me, my circle of friends began to shrink considerably. It is nice to know when your associates have less than good intentions in their relationship with you. Keep your observations to yourself. It is a little edge you have in communication. It even works over the phone.

The Kundalini enhances who you are. That's why you should really work on the secret smile. A positive attitude is not only good for your health but will allow you to deal with situations from a "What's best for all involved?" viewpoint. Seek out others who have actually gone through the process. Doc mentioned to me personally, only a handful of people who he knew had done it without going nuts and were able to articulate the experience. The rest who claim to have Kundalini awakened are mistaking chi development for the big bang. Our ego, which is designed to protect the body, will try to trick you into believing the id has emerged. If it truly allows the id to have a say then your ego will feel like it doesn't have control of your body. The Kundalini requires intense emotional states to awaken. I agree with Doc that there is no such thing as a partial Kundalini awakening. His article about this is in the back of this book. If someone is telling you they can help you activate your Kundalini, make sure they are credible. Doc lists the signs and symptoms of a true Kundalini survivor in his books. You may be in great danger if your "guru" is full of shit. Follow your heart or contact Tao, Santiago, James, Fudosan or me if you get fried and your helper can't fix the problem.

Chapter 6

Experiences with Busato Morris

The following are some of the interesting events that I had training and hanging out with Doc Morris. The events I describe are from those who were witness and my observation. I am not here to convince anyone of anything. I just share my perspective and answer questions from my experiences. Though most of what we do with chi can be classified as "weird science" as Doc called it, some of the things I witnessed are beyond the simple explanation of bioenergetics.

During a visit to the Hombu, Doc asked me what I wanted to work on. I told him I wanted to test for my Shodan in Hoshinjutsu. He stood in front of me and looked at my shoulders and up to my head. "Well, you have opened the lesser Kan and Li (microcosmic orbit); I can take you through Kundalini by the end of the week." I chickened out of letting him take me through the full awakening as I had to drive 850 miles home. He laughed. We changed and went outside to play. We reviewed the entire Hillsdale curriculum out of his original teaching notebook. Those who trained with him learned out of it. The red notebook with the original Hoshinjutsu and Hoshin

Tao Chi Kung patches glued to the front. He would ask me to show something and I would do it. We traded nasty strategies for a few hours. After a break Glenn walked over to me and said "I'm gonna hit ya." then immediately slammed his fist into my chest. I felt a blast of energy come in my chest and go out of my feet. It hurt so much. He looked at me funny and said "Huh, you took it. That hit usually drops people." I had a green and purple bruise for weeks.

We squared off again. I threw a punch at him and as he lifted his arm he waved his hand close to his chest, moving inside my punch. I felt his hand touch me softly and then my whole body flipped over and I was thrown onto my back. He stood over me chuckling as I got up. I asked him how he threw me. He said the kami (spirits) threw me. I have tried to play with repeating the technique but cannot not find a way to throw from the position he was in. We continued to scan the belt levels as Doc would ask me to explain things like the Godai, chi kung, martial dynamics vs. techniques and energy use for healing and combat. I already had some chi from doing the Hoshin Tao Chi Kung meditations for opening the micro and macrocosmic orbits. I had not tried for Kundalini up to that point.

After going through his entire notebook, I earned my Shodan in Hoshin Jutaijutsu. The notebook is also full of Glenn's favorite articles and research with his hand written notes and commentary on the sides. It contained the White belt through Godan manuals. Very few people have read those belt manuals as there were only a few 4th and 5th dan Hoshin practitioners at the time. Of those, maybe 2 were active teachers that I was aware of. The Godan or 5th dan manual goes into the spiritual guidance of students as well as reevaluation of your own development. Keeping the white belt attitude and always learning, as well as being open and honest with your students. Glenn's master notebook is full of interesting knowledge. I am blessed to have it now. I read through it often and it reminds me of what a genius we had in Doc.

Doc Morris liked to play hard. His body had been beaten by all sorts of accidents in sports, martial arts and car wrecks. I asked him if I could give him a massage and fix any issues. He happily said yes and he stripped down to his undies and got on the table. I started the session at the head of the table. I looked down at Doc and could tell his muscles were pulling his head a bit to the left. I performed the face and scalp massage then began a stretch under the base of his skull which releases the muscles of the head and neck. I could feel tingling in my hands and arm that seemed to be creeping up into my body. I was holding my finger tips under the base of his skull and pulling slowly. Glenn's body jerked from his neck to his feet then went back to totally relaxed again. My arms were on fire from it. I was nervous as hell. I calmly asked if he was alright. He said I had released an old blockage.

I continued to work on Doc as the fire eased and I began using this energy he was giving me in the session. I worked on all the areas of tension I could find. I glanced at the clock and I had worked on Glenn for 3 ½ hours. I usually do 90 min. sessions. He asked me if he was feeding me enough, meaning transmitting energy to me. I said yes and began the ending work of tapotement (slapping and percussive techniques for bringing energy to an area).

Later at dinner we were discussing shakitpat and how one can be "sparked off" by an awakened master. Glenn said "The energy you give to someone will change them. At the same time, you receive energy from them also and must always be aware and disperse excess energy. You can send it into the ground or cycle it in your orbit and "eat" the energy if you like how it feels."

I asked Doc how long it would take to awaken my Kundalini if he gave me a mega boost and he said, "It will happen depending on how much you meditate." He looked at me and smiled and said, "It's too late for you, (laughing) I have infected you and it will work its way through. The more you meditate the sooner you will pop. But it will happen." I felt a wave of nervousness mixed with disbelief that it could really work that simply. That night Glenn verbally guided me through the Kundalini awakening meditations and the Taoist flaming sword meditations for healing, fighting and drawing power from the elements, along with a couple that were transmitted to me as oral tradition from master to deshi.

Doc liked to go hiking. When he lived in Lake Charles he would take his visiting friends to the bayou to see the gators. We drove out to New Iberia, right along the coast of the swamp. We got out of the car and Doc sprayed me down with a military grade mosquito repellant. As we walked toward the edge of the swamp there were huge mosquitoes that swarmed in unbelievable numbers. We were brushing hundreds of them off each other's back as we walked a small path that went between the river bends. After about 50 yards into the bayou the mosquitoes disappeared. It was like they had a barrier from the outside edge of the swamp. We walked deeper into the swamp as snakes and baby gators slithered by.

I happened upon a large gator sitting on the river bank. He was about 6 feet and thick. He had been eating well. I got as close as could without feeling like the croc hunter and examined this beast, who could kill me if I got too close. I took a picture and backed away. Glenn had walked across a narrow foot bridge that was about 40 feet long. He was already on the other side looking out into the water. I noticed a brownish cloud coming up the river from my left. As it approached I realized it was a swarm of wasps.

Glenn had told me about the Louisiana wasps that were huge yellow jackets. They had a powerful sting. I felt uneasy as they collected into a sphere shaped swarm between Doc and me, over the bridge. I thought back to when I first walked fire. I assumed the go for it attitude and, with no fear and great confidence, walked across the bridge through this swarm of wasps. They were bouncing off my face and body as I walked through them to the other side of the bridge. I didn't get stung. I walked over to Doc with adrenaline pumping through me. I turned and looked back to see the swarm circle, break formation and fly on down the river. I asked Doc if he had seen the swarm and he didn't answer. He suggested we get moving before it got dark and the real critters came out to feed. He was such a wizard. He was testing me using familiars in nature. I posted to the ryu list about it and another guy who had a similar experience on the bridge replied. He had been stung. Doc never addressed it. It was his way of testing us. Glad I passed that one.

During another visit to Soke Morris I was practicing the standing stake meditations for developing Jing chi. I was about 20 minutes into the practice when I heard a soft Asian woman's voice whispering to me. I couldn't understand her and found it quite strange that I was actually hearing a voice. Usually, I would receive spirit messages through empathy. The messages were never audible. I thought that's what happens to crazy people, hearing voices. I asked who was speaking to me and I heard her say "Quan Yin." I asked again and heard the same thing again. I finished my session and went to Glenn, who was sitting at his computer answering emails. I asked him if he had ever heard of Quan Yin. His eyes got big and he said "Quan Yin, consider yourself lucky! I have been trying to get on her wavelength for years. She usually appears to great healers." I never heard any audible voices after that. Glenn was tickled I had been visited at his house.

I attended the McNesse State University graduation with Doc one year. He was sitting with the other professors and I made my way up to the stadium seats. I was sitting there feeling all of the emotions from the families. There were students graduating with doctorates and the pride emanating from the auditorium was thick. I said to myself that I wished the lights were a bit dimmer so that I could see the auras around the family members watching their loved ones graduate. A few minutes later all the lights went out in the building. I sat in darkness, looking at the glowing coronas surrounding the families. A few minutes later the backup lights came on and everyone found their seat. Soon the main auditorium lights were back on and the graduation ceremony continued. After the ceremony was over I met Doc in the parking lot near his car. He asked me "You do that...to the lights?" I explained that I wanted to see the auras of the parents and families of the graduates. He said "You have to be careful with this stuff. Chi is powerful. I thought it was you." It was a hell of a coincidence. I had blown out light bulbs and blown fuses before but nothing of this scale. Glenn's wife at the time lectured me on the responsibility that comes with chi development. I learned to think ahead of my desires. There is always karma to keep us in check.

In February of 2002 my student Chris Robinson and I went to visit Soke Morris. Glenn had assigned me the task of working on Systema and learning the principles of their movements. We were there to show Doc what I had learned. One evening, while Chris was cooking dinner and I was preparing to give Doc a massage, the phone rang. Doc answered and after a few words handed me the phone and said "It's for you." My father was on the phone and he asked me to sit down. "Are you sitting down?" he said. "Yes, what's going on?" I replied. "Your mom committed suicide this morning," he responded.

I was in disbelief. She had survived three heart attacks, colon cancer surgery and was dealing with severe fibromyalgia. Normally, when you hear someone has done something bad, you imagine their consequences. I began to realize that there were no consequences. My mother was dead. I got off the phone and stood up, feeling a mixture of anger and an overwhelming sadness. I looked at Doc and told him the news. I was welling up with tears. Glenn gave me a big hug, then turned me around and began vibrating his hands up my spine and brushing the energy away. It was amazing what began to happen. My emotions began to settle and my sadness disappeared. He gave me a few good pats and asked if I was ok.

Somehow, Glenn had stopped my emotions from overtaking me. I was in a state of melancholy, like I had taken a drug that wouldn't let me be sad. I remember giving Glenn his massage while I thought of what had occurred. The amazing thing was that I was ok. It was as though I understood the grand scheme of things. It was a feeling of awe and comfort. Chris and I left the next day to go to my parent's house. The strange part is that as we drove away from Doc, my emotions slowly began to well up again. By the time we had left Lake Charles, I was a wreck.

Chris and I arrived at my mom and dad's house in South Carolina. Chris was tired and asked to nap for a few hours. I sat in the living room and talked with my father. I turned and looked down the hall toward her bedroom, which now looked like a crime scene. I was compelled to walk back there and see what, if anything, I would feel. I closed my eyes and felt her emotions, her pain and fear. I saw in my mind's eye the whole thing. It was almost too much. I opened my eyes and walked back out and sat with my family.

Once Chris awoke he told me that while he had been lying half asleep, he felt someone come in and stand near the bed. They seemed confused and didn't recognize who he was. My mom had only seen him once. He said he saw what looked like a heart, surrounded by white lace appear in his third eye. Loving feelings came over him and a sense of comfort.

Before we left, I walked into the room again and told to my mom if she felt lost or trapped she could ride home with me and I would send her in the right direction. I inhaled and drew in the energy in the room. Once I was home, I went into meditation and attempted communication. The message was this: My mom, who feared dying of cancer, had decided to take her life. She attempted to overdose on pills Valentine's Day evening, throwing them up and shot herself the day after. This was later verified. She hung out with me for a few days until she understood that her work here was done. She moved on towards the light and her next adventure. Sometimes, spiritual ability can test ones sanity and be emotionally taxing. Especially when it's a loved one you are interacting with. Another reason the secret smile should be mastered before your empathic ability develops.

My Personal Observations of Doc

The first time I met Doc in person, I was amazed by how he looked. His aura was bright white and the area surrounding his head and shoulders looked like it was fuzzy or out of focus. I had been able to see auras for years and his was the brightest I had ever seen. You could feel him as he walked toward you. Like a static electric sensation. The man had a serious amount of juice.

Doc was his own man. He didn't change his persona based on the environment. He was the same with his friends, family and faculty. He had a brother, but rarely talked about his family. He loved his family. But alas, he loved Hoshin more. When push came to shove on the home front, unfortunately for some and fortunately for others, Hoshin would always win out. If you ever had the opportunity to spend time one-on-one with Doc at his house you probably would have played a game of chess or two. Doc loved to play chess. He was above average in his play. He never played in any tournaments, just for the pleasure of spending time with his Hoshin friends.

In addition to being a university professor in speech he worked with corporate training, primarily on BOMC upper management. After leaving Hillsdale College he started his own corporate training company. Using the principles of the Godai and the MAPS Inventory, he was able to secure several corporate contracts. He would work with corporations on soft skills like teamwork, time management, and how to hire the right employees using the principles of Hoshin.

I do not know all the friends that Doc had in his life time, but I do know most of the friends he had in the last decade of his life. This is easy, because most of his friends were Hoshin students. The one constant in the second half of Docs life was martial arts, and particularly Hoshin. He would rely on the members as much as they relied on him. If he ever had a problem, he would immediately look to the professional skills of the Hoshin members for help rather than turn to the yellow pages. He enjoyed having Hoshin students stay and train with him, sometimes weeks or even months at a time. He would open his house to any and all Hoshin members wanting to stay with him. There have been several seminars at or near his house; where there were so many students staying at his house that there was hardly any floor space to walk.

Doc's compassion allowed him to build relationships with his familiars. While living in Lake Charles, Doc had a spider that would build a web under the canapé of his backdoor each night. In the morning when Doc would exit his house he would run into the spider web, essentially destroying most of its structure. Then one day Doc had a talk with the spider on compromising the formation of the web. The next morning when Doc came out of his house the spider web was still there, however, the spider designed an arch in the web exactly where Doc walked and exactly at Doc's height.

Doc was simple in his choice of foods. He would prefer to share a loaf of bread and a bottle of wine, over a fancy French five course dinner. He was a great cook. His signature spaghetti sauce 'Dr. Death's nuclear spaghetti sauce' would test any spice lover's heat tolerance. He loved to surprise his guests with new tastes. The first time I had anchovies was when I asked Doc to order us a pizza. I was buying, but told him to get what he liked. They weren't bad. Since visiting Glenn in Louisiana I get a craving for gumbo and blackberry wine now and then. Energy exchange can be funny when you get a taste for something you don't normally desire.

I have to say that the most endearing and memorable part of Doc was his smile. Throughout his teachings he talks about the secret smile. But for Doc, his smile was no secret. His smile was about the joy in embracing life. He would smile when he was happy, when he thought of or heard of a brilliant idea, or when life just crashed in on him.

Glenn had been screwed over by more than one of his associates. Some wanted their own system; adding Glenn's Hoshin Tao Chi Kung to whatever they were doing and disregarded his Hoshin Jutaijutsu. Some Glenn had put money up to help invest in their dojo and was never paid back. Some just wanted to be a Grandmaster themselves. This always pissed me off as it seemed like stealing. Some of these people were actually using Doc to promote themselves and broke away to found their own systems. Glenn would say "Imitation is the greatest form of flattery. Just wait till they have to develop chi in others. They either got it or they don't. Most who stray eventually come back."

Doc believed in the traditional relationships expressed in Budo. I was with him and Chris Robinson at the local market shopping for groceries. Doc looked at Chris (Who was a Water Belt at the time) and told him he wanted a cup of coffee. Chris asked him what kind he liked and went over to get us all a cup. Doc had grabbed a fresh baked loaf of French bread at the bakery. We sat down to enjoy our coffee and Glenn tore off a hunk of bread, passed the loaf to me and said to Chris "No bread for the kohai." I looked at Chris who was starving from all the training we had been doing, tore off a piece for him, and then tore off a piece for me. I handed the rest of the loaf back to Doc and he smiled. It was Doc's way of showing whose student Chris was. Hierarchy was unimportant to Soke Morris, yet he showed it to serious students. After Fire belt, you are considered part of the inner circle of Hoshin. You earn the right, as rank has its privileges.

I had the honor of watching Doc perform as Boo Radley in a stage performance of *To Kill a Mockingbird*. It was performed at the Little Theatre in Lake Charles, La., one of the oldest theatres in the country. The first night I went to watch the play. The second night I videotaped it from a booth above the crowd. He had very few lines, yet his acting and body movements embodied the scared outcast who would be the subject of town ridicule in the story. It was a side of Glenn that I feel very lucky to have experienced. I can still see him huddled behind the barn, looking out with fear and anxiety. He was great at assuming a role. This was one of the best times I ever had watching Glenn. He truly loved the theatre. That was his passion. He definitely knew how to work a crowd.

Chapter 7

Empathic Communication

I don't hang out in the void all the time or go looking for entities. Let me state that normally the way I "talk" to these energy beings is through sharing energy with a message attached. I usually catch any energy changes in my immediate surroundings. I can feel that something is there. If I am interested, I can tune into it then inhale the energy of it to feel the intent. Feelings emerge that convey a message based on the intentions. Imagine someone told you that you won the lottery. How would you feel? Excited? In, awe?

Now picture being able to receive the message and feeling without being spoken to. This is what empathic communication is like. It feels like a conversation without words. You give and receive energy for as long as your level of ability will allow. If the exchange begins to feel forced or ugly, either drop the tongue and seal off your throat chakra, or disconnect your tongue from the normal spot and inhale all the energy in front of you. Run it in around the orbit until it burns up. If it is too much to handle, go outside in the grass or bare ground and push the energy/being into the ground. Once you feel it all go out, step away from the spot. I have only had to do that a few times. Having a body seems to be a great advantage. They usually run if you threaten to eat them. I will sometimes see them as a light or distortion in my normal vision. This will range from whizzing lights to shadows in motion. They want you to notice. It might take a tremendous amount of energy for them to manifest, even for just a moment. If they are bound to a certain location, sustained image could be possible. This may explain why ghosts that haunt a certain place are seen more often. If they attach themselves to an individual, they may feed and exchange energy. The person may have no idea.

Random thoughts seem to emerge that are unorthodox to your normal thinking. These thoughts will usually bring about an emotional response. This is where the energy exchange happens. The emotion attached to your minds response carry energy. In a trained and aware individual, these exchanges can become relationships. This is referred to as spirit guides. The more you feed energy to it, the more it shares. Energy exchange is not a one way street, even for vampires. If you give, you will get. The same is true if you take energy from someone. The thoughts, feeling and mind set is passed between participants. This can be seen in every type of relationship. Be it married couples, teachers and students or spirit guides. To Roshi (spirit masters), these spirits can become workers or pets, depending on skill level. I have seen devout Christians drive away "demons" with their faith and intention. It seems that the names we give to our deities are a focal point for intention. The universe lends its helping hand to those with conviction. Some say Jesus, others say God and Goddess but the source seems to be the same and the effects of calling on divine intervention almost identical.

I have seen a few cases where nasty critters seemed to be tormenting their host. One of the most memorable was the case of my student Robb Furr's girlfriend. Robb called me and said he had a serious problem and needed my advice. His girlfriend was being attacked by some sort of entity. I went to her house with Robb and we all sat at the kitchen table to discuss what was happening. I had never met her before. She stated that at random intervals this being would press or sit on her making her unable to move. I had never seen anything that severe, just the usual haunting with noise and things moving around during the night.

As we continued to talk I saw the young girls face go white and she began to tear up. I asked "Are you ok?" She answered, "It's here." "Where is it?" I replied. "Sitting in my lap!" she cried.

I stood up and walked over to her side. Robb stood on the other side of her and we grabbed her by the arms and tried to lift her up. We couldn't budge her. She was crying hysterically at this point. I had seen my folk's Pentecostal minister use Jesus' name to drive away ugly spirits. I started praying out loud and asked heaven to help drive this nasty thing away. It wasn't budging so I commanded in Jesus' name that it leave and it flew off her lap and down the hall and out a window. I did a protective prayer to block it from returning. I now understand that because I had been raised to believe that the name Jesus could drive away evil, it gave me the strength and conviction to scare it away. I later came to understand that my faith or intention could be given any name and would bring out the power within. This is how Psionics work. We each have beliefs that are sacred to us. My advice is to cherish your faith. Just try not to alienate those of other faiths. It's a free country. If you argue over religious views you appear to be of weak faith. If you are happy and believe in your religious views, why argue with someone from the "My religion is better than yours!" viewpoint. Don't demonize what you fear or are just ignorant of. I suggest a book on cultural anthropology. Reading about other religions will either solidify your own beliefs or spark interest in other paths. There is a great similarity in most of the major religions in the world.

The Kundalini is hidden deep in the mythology of practically every culture. It is cross cultural and is repressed information in most belief systems. The Kundalini is truly biological, yet it causes spiritual insights that could create an entire belief system. It is no wonder that without social limitations, ancient cultures could have gone off the deep end after their leaders were opened to Kundalini Shakti and the universal consciousness. Some cultures have practices that we call strange, yet to them it is ultimate faith. I don't agree with the ones who take pride in killing their enemies, especially through their own demise. Suicide bomber takes superhuman faith, or stupidity. History is truly written by the winners. The wars continue even today over the simplest of concepts, faith.

It is true what Doc said about the spirits eventually merging with the individual. If you are using a mirror to "see" your kindred spirits, over time they will be harder to draw out as a separate apparition. They become a part of you. In meditation they can be felt in close proximity to the body.

If you are practicing the Damo's cave exercise your spirit guides may occupy a room in your cave. I didn't know what my guides looked like until I saw them in this way. In the dojo in my cave I would train with a young samurai. His hair is pulled back and he wears loose canvas clothing. He is close to my age and teaches with humor. Every once in a while, an older warrior will pop in and tell us we are having too much fun. He is the serious side of budo and keeps us focused. I also have a huge armored samurai who is my protector and has a very nasty temper. When I meditate, I can feel them sitting with me. The young warrior sits just behind and to the right of me, the old master behind him, and the protector behind and to the left.

One time while meditating, I felt something coming through the wall from my neighbor's townhouse. It floated over towards me and seemed curious. My angry samurai jumped up and growled at it like a guard dog. The energy backed away and went home. It was like "Oh shit, wrong place!" My new neighbor was a young Wiccan woman who was probably practicing her astral projection to see what was going on at my place. She avoided me after that.

My student Chris Robinson had caught the attention of my big samurai during mirror trick practice. I was showing how to draw out spirit guides and this one decided to follow him home. He called from his driveway and said that some huge figure was in his house, looking at him through the kitchen window. I was only a few miles away and said I would be right over. He explained that while sitting in meditation at his house this "thing" was floating above his head, distracting him during his session. I met him outside and asked him to unlock the door so I could go in first. He followed close behind. I walked up the steps, down the hall and around the corner to a back guest room. I saw him floating in the far left corner of the room. I told him to leave Chris alone. Chris was surprised that I had walked right to where the spirit was. He had not told me where in the house he would meditate and there were several rooms. I explained that my samurai had probably felt me think something like, "I want Chris to get better at Hoshin", and decided to hang out with him. I learned that my guides could be loaned to students who struggled with techniques or chi development. They can be sent on errands or to check up on friends and loved ones. You must feed them to keep them around.

I was asked to come to Ft. Lauderdale to help promote the Kundalini Awakening Process seminars with Doc. Santiago Dobles and Tao Semko were at the expo and we all sat together in our booth. We talked with many people about the KAP program and Kundalini in general. I was Glenn's poster boy; the guy who didn't totally lose his mind and could articulate his experience to others. We had a copy of the KAP manual that we were showing diagrams from as we explained what we were teaching and why one would want to do it. Doc and I gave free chakra balancing to folks while "the boys" answered questions.

We were preparing to break for lunch when Glenn asked "Where is our manual?" It had been sitting on the table next to the registration sheet. No one remembered it disappearing. I decided to put one of my guides to work. I said "I will send a spirit helper to go get it back."

I made a mental sweep of the huge convention center we were in and pushed out my samurai to go find it. After about 15 minutes a very flustered woman walked over to our booth and said "I can't take your course. I got a splitting headache a few minutes after I left your booth." She laid the manual down and walked away. Doc leaned over and gave me a stern look. I said "It's the only copy we have!" He broke into hysterical laughter. The visitors hanging out at our booth were shocked. Doc treated it as though it was no big deal. I forget sometimes that not very many share our interests. It seems to scare the living shit out of most people.

Chapter 8

Politics and Mayhem

As with most families, Hoshin has had its share of characters and events, which, although at the time were trying, have since integrated into the lore and legend of the ryu.

In the summer of 2003, Glenn had enlisted the help of a guy, who will remain nameless here, to help promote Hoshin into a successful business. The guy gets on our ryu members list and starts telling us all how he is running a real business for Doc and that we all have to listen to him. After basically pissing off most of the instructors and not giving respect where it is due, we began to get concerned that this person had his own interests, not Glenn's in mind. An apparent takeover seemed to be happening. Shortly after all this was going on, Glenn realized that the new "helper" was planning to incorporate in his own name, thus becoming the legal owner of Hoshinroshiryu. Dr. John Porter, a long time friend of Glenn's and a successful nonprofit organization CEO, approached Glenn about the legal means with which a takeover could occur. It was decided that the Hoshinroshiryu would be registered in John's name and he would work with Doc to create a business structure for the ryu. Once John registered the ryu with the IRS and had all of the business plan mapped out, he contacted Doc and asked that we arrange a meeting to get the business rolling. Doc, John and I met for dinner to discuss the details. The federal EIN number confirmation and a business and marketing plan were presented. The plan was that Dr. Porter would get the business up and running for Doc, then make him executive director after a few years. The "helper" was excused and actually wrote an email to another chat list just before Glenn passed away stating that Doc was a fake. After he found out about Glenn's passing, he wrote a rebuttal.

Doc and I continued to work together at standardizing the Hoshinjutsu curriculum. I finished the Hoshin Healing certification program and set up a distance training program for it with manuals and DVDs of the healing techniques. Doc would say that people get more practice at using energy for healing than fighting. I founded the Hoshin Budo Association which was my network of instructors and students for the Southeastern U.S. During this time many other lesser known areas of study were being developed into formal programs for the ryu, including Hoshin Mikkyo, Mandala Therapy and Psionics training developed by Dr. John Porter and KAP with Santiago Dobles and Tao Semko of UMAA Tantra. These programs are offered through the Hoshinbudoryu.

While visiting Dr. Porter in West Chester, Ohio he asked me to go for a walk with him. We set out into the night and discussed the Hoshin ryu, its current state and where it was headed. John informed me that Doc and he had discussed the future of Hoshin after Glenn's retirement. I was told that my name had been brought up and that they had agreed that I would be the best choice for successor. The plan was to get the ryu going as a real business and when Doc decided to retire I would run the show. It was a great honor to hear him saying all this. I didn't like thinking about Doc retiring. I told John that Hoshin was my life and I would do my best to keep it going. I was so humbled by all of it. Glenn had been a guide and teacher to me and I love him like a father. I have survived my best and worst times with his advice. He would always be straight and to the point. A few months later while on the phone with Doc he said, "Once I retire, I want you running the show. I consider you my next of kin. I know Shawn doesn't want to fool with it. You have all the good stuff. Kundalini, Hoshinjutsu and you are a healer. I have been looking for you for a while…Are we happy?" I told Glenn that I was honored and that I would strive to keep Hoshin growing. It was understood that I wouldn't discuss this with anyone. Glenn told me he trusted me and I had worked hard for him. "Now, never screw me over! Once I decide to retire you will be the man."

I continued to teach and promote students in Hoshin just as I had. I kept my mouth shut. Glenn would occasionally make a comment around other people about me being the next soke. It slipped out in a small circle at Not the Kai Zen in 2004. Kenny Sutton caught it but didn't say anything at the time. He had also mentioned it around Chris Robinson, my top student who would visit Doc with me. He eventually told more people including James Alexander, Santiago Dobles, other students and a few ninja associates who had friends that were training with me.

On April 1st 2006, I received a call from Doug Tweedy. Doug asked if I had heard the news about Doc. Kenny Sutton, a ninja friend from Kentucky had called him saying he was not sure of the details, but was told Glenn had passed away. I got off the phone with Doug and called Kenny. He said once he got the word for sure he would call me back. He called back a few minutes later. It was true.

I had just spoken to Doc in March and his last words to me were, "I think I am ready to retire, I never recovered very well from my broken leg (in 2002) and am just too old to get beat on." I told him that Hoshin would continue just as it had and that he didn't have to worry. I had worked hard to get the Ninpo out of the belt manuals and the core Hoshin was finally organized. The advanced belts new info was ready and we were poised to get it out to the world.

The official announcement came to the ryu list later that day. I was in shock and left work. I had lost my friend, mentor and the best teacher I had ever had. Everyone took time to reflect and shared stories and what they loved about Doc. Folks began asking about the future and who would be the next Hoshin soke. It was stated on the ryu list that explicit instructions had been left and that the new soke would be announced at the 2006 Kai Zen in July.

John Porter, being the executive director of the Hoshinroshiryu, asked that a copy of the letter be sent to him or that the name be made public. If there was not a letter proving Glenn's wishes, the ryu members and instructors would put it to a vote. Dr. Porter nominated me as acting soke. He also requested that any other nominations for soke of the ryu be submitted along with their training qualifications, at which time the most senior members of the ryu would review the soke candidate resumes and select the best candidate.

A few days later there was an unexpected announcement from Irena Morris that the new soke of Hoshinroshiryu was Gord Hessie. It was then stated that explicit instructions had been left by Glenn. Gord was very surprised. He contacted me and we discussed the announcement. Gord Hessie is a man of great character. I had met him in 2004 at the Not the Kai Zen in West Chester, Ohio. I led the fire walk ceremony that year which was also his first time embracing the embers! He is very nice and easy to talk to, a good guy.

A student of mine had sent me an email (see index) that I had forwarded to them a year earlier. The email, written in 2005, was Glenn's response to Gord regarding where to seek out Hoshin training. In the email Glenn wrote, "You should get that piece of the puzzle from him (me). I consider him my successor." Glenn had sent the email to Gord and me. At the time, it blew me away to see him telling other people, but he was very outspoken around people he liked.

The student who sent me the email was very upset over the announcement and told me that they would not accept a Hoshin soke that had not awakened Kundalini. Other black belts of mine began to share similar feeling. They asked me to get them a copy of the letter so they could see it for themselves. I was being contacted by folks I didn't know who were telling me Glenn had named me to run his ryu. I was so frustrated. I wanted to simply keep Hoshin going and forget all the political bullshit. It is, after all, the art that is important.

I decided to keep my mouth shut and see what would happen. Hell, I was still grieving over Doc's passing and all the political shit was not helping things. I sent the email to Gord to see if he remembered it. I called him up and explained what was happening in my training groups. Gord wanted to be sure that the letter indeed existed. He traveled to Lake Charles, La. where he searched through Glenn's file cabinets and piles of papers and documents. He did not find a letter.

Being a man of honor, Gord contacted me and suggested that we let the members vote on who they wanted to be soke. I was the moderator of the Hoshinroshiryu email list, where emotions were running very high. Ryu members were discussing the silent behind the scene nature of the situation. After personal attacks began between ryu members with differences in opinions, Gord called me and suggested that we just make everyone happy and run separate Hoshin ryu. I decided that since my network was named Hoshin Budo Association I would be Hoshinbudoryu. Gord made the announcement to the ryu list and I followed with my own response. It was a win/win solution.

A year later Glenn's widow Irena called me and we had a very nice talk about everything that had transpired. She apologized to me for having messed anything up. There were people telling her different things and she knows nothing about martial arts. She stated that she recognizes both schools and is proud of the work we are doing. She was only 25 when Glenn passed, having to deal with the loss of a loved one, funeral arrangements, financial and legal arrangements and a ryu of people asking her what to do. At the time of this writing Irena is facing deportation from the US under the widow penalty. The law states that if a person is married to a US citizen who dies before they have been married 2 years, the immigrant's citizenship is removed. I find it ridiculous that although she attended college at McNesse, she lost her citizenship after being married and widowed. She is part of Second Life, an online network of artists and graphic designers who create assumed identities, her name is Eshi Otawara.

Her custom dresses are like something out of a fairytale. They are truly unique and elegant, in a Gothic fantasy sort of way. She created her Second Life virtual avatar to look like Doc. She has made virtual simulations with Glenn flying and exploring the outdoors. Her paintings convey a real world sense. Some are of intense scenes of war or holocaust. I like the portrait she did of her and Glenn. She painted a picture of a spider, using Glenn's ashes mixed in the paint. Kevin Millis presented it to Hatsumi on her behalf. I'm sure he loved it. Glenn was posthumously given his Judan (10th degree black belt) and the title of Shihan in Bujinkan Budo Taijutsu by Soke Hatsumi.

Chapter 9

Testimonials from Students and Friends

The following are testimonials from students and friend whom I have trained with extensively. They share my interest in learning the esoteric aspects of martial arts mastery. The testimonials are in no particular order. I have learned a great deal from each of these individuals. Here is what they had to say about me.

"I've been involved in Martial Arts for most of my life, Power Lifting, Tae Kwon Do, JKD, BJJ, Boxing, Wrestling, MMA and of course Hoshin. I have had the opportunity to learn from professional fighters, members of the All Marine Wrestling and Boxing Teams; as mastery is a lifelong pursuit and the goal is in the journey. I have trained with, deployed, and served alongside some of the greatest warriors on the face of the planet, the United States Marine. I have had multiple attempts on my life along with the lives of my fellow sailors and marines while serving duty in Iraq.

It was 1993 when I met Glenn for the first time. I had picked up a copy of *Path Notes* in October of that year, and read it straight through that night. I had been looking for something more in my personal development as a fighter and human, and *Path Notes* had the answer. I actually tracked Dr. Morris down via phone and we began a dialog and relationship that would last for over ten years . . . ending in April 2006 when he left us to live in the void. Dr. Morris gave freely of his time and expertise, even though he would throw a riddle in the mix every now and then.

It would be six years before I actually met him in person and I did just that in January of 1999 when I spent three days with him at his place in Houston TX. We talked, trained, and meditated. We looked at Hatsumi videos and got to play with Shidoshi Dave Bolin and his group of Ninjas. When I left Glenn, I had a better understanding of Energy, and life in general. I really miss the guy. I had the opportunity to see him again in July of that same year at a seminar in Eugene, Oregon. He was pleased by my development and had the group look at my Aura and recommended to them to not even try and fight me but just shoot me instead. We had a great time and he and his wife at the time actually met my wife at the time and they did a great deal to explain and show that Hoshin esoteric training is not worshiping the devil or any of that stuff. We are just a bunch of people that train to be the best warriors, healers and human beings that we could be. It was sad that the seminar had to end.

At this point, I had been in the United States Navy since 1989. I was stationed in Long Beach, California. I then left Long Beach in 1995 to be stationed on the USS Lincoln (Air Craft Carrier). In 1998, I left the Lincoln to be stationed at the Naval Hospital in Bremerton, Washington. In 2001, I was commissioned as Naval Officer and a lot of what I accomplished by finishing my College education, working hard and staying focused was due to what Glenn had taught me. I was to leave Washington State to come to the great state of

North Carolina. Before I left, Glenn directed me to find a guy by the name of Rob Williams. Dr. Morris stated that "this guy is not like you" (Yang). "He's a Yin guy and has trained in old school Bujinkan, and you will like him. He can show you how to work the magic." Glenn was right; I met Soke Williams in August of 2001 and liked him immediately. Glenn was also right that we are different, Rob is about 170lb and I am about 225lbs. But, our personal lives share a great deal of similarities almost to an uncanny degree.

It was almost humorous when we would get together because all of a sudden, he would get hot and want to turn on the air conditioner and open all the windows, and I would want to turn the heat on and close all of the windows. We trained, meditated and Rob demonstrated energy skills, such as fighting with chi, empty force and bending a candle flame. Sometimes we would be outside, some times in. At times the weather would be extremely cold and at other times it would be very hot. Rain, sleet, in the dark, blind folded while avoiding the sword, we did it all. I still scratch my head at times when I see this guy move.

Here it is 2007, 14 years after I first read *Path Notes*, six years after I began training with Rob and one year after Soke Morris' passing. A lot of changes have taken place within Hoshin. I had predicted and foreseen some of these changes ten years ago. There is no question as to where my loyalties lie. The Hoshin Budo Ryu is dedicated to keeping Glenn's legacy alive and is continuing to evolve. Soke Williams easily fills the shoes of our founder... and then some."

James Alexander
Lieutenant United States Navy
Shihan, Hoshinbudoryu

June, 2005

"While preparing for a class down on the north bank of the York River, in the state of Virginia, I made a call to the Hoshin soke, Rob Williams. I had read his teachers published works; Path notes, Shadow Strategies and Martial Madness. I wanted to take the chance to look in to the practice of Hoshin while the opportunity presented itself close at hand. At that time, Rob Williams was not the Hoshin soke and his teacher was still present in the world. I arranged to call on him during my time in the area, to which he was open and amenable.

I spent the days in the classroom away from the dry hot heat of those days on the north bank of the river, and retreated to my hotel during the evenings preparing for next day's classes. I called upon Mr. Williams and arranged a convenient time that we could discuss his art and how practice was conducted. So I crossed the bridge to the south bank of the York River and made my way according to his direction to his place of residence one evening after sundown.

At this point I should diverge and explain something of myself as a reference point. I was thirty one years of age, a veteran of the navy and dropout of the SEAL program. I have studied martial arts since I was seven starting with YMCA karate, moving on to a McTae Kwon Do school later in my middle and high school years. Finally I had been kicking around in Aikido dojos for years on the east coast of the U.S. and some in Japan and spending the last couple of years looking at Hatsumi-den budo taijutsu.

I had never attained a black belt rank up to that point. I have been around and trained with some talented martial artists, spent some time with elite special operations people while involved in SEAL training and even rubbed elbows with a few dangerous thugs. In addition, I have attended Qigong and Yichuan classes that assert matter of fact knowledge of bioelectrical living energy.

I arrived at the house of this martial artist with martial arts and the material in his teachers books foremost on my mind. Having been so enthusiastically encouraged by the conversation we had on the phone I was easily able to put all martial considerations of the strategic aspects of our first meeting aside. He greeted me on the front stoop, the porch light blaring behind him casting him completely in shadow; I could not make out anything about him except for a wide smile and a shaven head. I think I may have shuddered a moment before shaking it off and extending my hand in greeting. It was after all 'all good'!

During that first meeting we talked about a many aspects of martial training like two old buddies sharing stories and perspectives which was no surprise. It was encouraging to meet a new friend; however Rob Williams is more than that. He is a teacher of self protection and self study. The now Hoshin soke, quickly showed me various basic energy work, some of which I had experienced, but none of which had remained easily reproducible when I was alone. So I was easily convinced of the validity of what he was doing, especially because of the intensity at which I was able to easily feel the level of energetic display of what Mr. Williams was showing.

We discussed martial applications and training all of which was in alignment with my usual ideas. So I was inspired and motivated to continue to seek out Hoshin practice. He talked about his fondness and thankfulness for all he had received from his teacher. Not wanting to take up too much of his time I politely thanked him and excused myself. It was made clear I was welcome to come back, and I accepted his invitation.

Summer and Fall, 2005

Twice a week, I made the hour long trek from Richmond, Virginia to Yorktown, Virginia to train. The next time I saw him he had moved to a different location and during the afternoons there was a wide open space available to his classes behind his house. I met some of his students, who were all involved only with his school. Encouraged by this new place to train I would bring friends to train with the Hoshin group.

Very quickly I fell into the role of student, and Mr. Williams is very serious about perpetuating the Hoshin ryu of his teacher. Soke Williams is an unassuming character of simple kind straightforward courtesy and humility. He believes in and supports through his teaching style the Hoshin ryu purpose of attempting to remove the shroud of mystery surrounding the sort of details that are usually reserved for the oral tradition among more secretive esoteric schools. This is evident in the Hoshin curriculum where a whole technique may be only a properly placed shove to completely foul up the balance of an opponent, a proper breathing method to maximize a desired effect or even a diagram for movement.

In other schools where these would be considered adjunct to technique, in Hoshin by contrast these are considered intrinsic. There is to a large degree an oral transmission that takes place, for example in the beginning levels the Hoshin soke went over the general principles of combat anatomy, bones, joints, glands and blood vessels. All this he does with great familiarity and without referencing any written material. This in and of itself may not be unusual for some combat systems, however when arriving at certain topics Hoshin Soke will add little side anecdotes of unusual variety and seemingly impossible plausibility. For instance the ability to momentarily immobilize an opponent's extended arm by simply moving the hand in front of the opponent. For me this was quite out of the ordinary, but can be verified, reproduced by anyone and once seen logically connected to simple concepts we already know to be true. So if offered, once the material is covered the only way to cover the material again is to be at a class when he is teaching that level to someone else, so this is what the current of information is like in Hoshin.

Conclusion

When talking about energy and its concomitants with regard to martial arts, healing and spirituality there is no end to the enthusiasm to which you will be greeted by interested parties who have only the merest inkling of experience. Hoshin soke treats it all with a grain of salt, though has an open door policy for those of serious inquiry.

I have compared a regular metal pen before and after he loaded it with chi through his hand, the weight difference was significant. I have seen him push or pull people with energy from a distance of more than twelve feet (and seen the hair of someone being pulled lift off of their back, before they were pulled).

After receiving a minor but intense bruise (seen and felt), Hoshin soke shrank it to almost nothing and felt icy cool air rushing from around his fanning hands on the surface of my skin. The fact is that this is just a beginning, but it should be enough. Rob Williams, soke does not stand to say that Hoshin is the only martial art that is of value, to offer proof that energy applications work or exist, but as the keeper of the Hoshin tradition passed on to him by the first Hoshin soke. Those that wish to learn something of that tradition are welcome. I feel a strong sense of gratitude for his sharing way and his friendship."

Paul Bernhard, DEC 21st, 2006

"My path is similar to many who have traveled in search of a Martial Arts Master. I spent a few years in Shorin-Ryu under a great Sensei who taught me discipline as well as how to generate power in my movements. No regrets, however I would always attend other seminars in the search of missing components that would supplement my training. In 2000 I was a few years into Hapkido when an acquaintance mentioned over dinner that he was training with someone in Yorktown. I asked the style and got a rambling dissertation on Hoshin and its origins. Mystical, deadly, effective, easy to duplicate.... Skeptical? You bet!

As I approached Rob, who at the time was central area Head of the Southeastern Hoshin Dojos, I found that he wasn't 7 foot tall and breathing fire but a pleasant looking young man wearing Birkenstocks. Looks can be deceiving and after training for 4 hours I rode home battered and bruised thinking I would have preferred the 7 foot tall fire breather! Hoshinjutsu embodied all that I was searching for and not only filled the holes in my martial training but set me down a path towards self actualization.

I met Soke Morris during a training trip Rob organized to Lake Charles, Louisiana. Rob was asked to come down and revamp the Hoshin Curriculum by Doc and I had the pleasure to be the uke for both of them as they shared techniques and strategies. During that trip Doc explained the hierarchy of his marital art and said that Rob was top amongst his instructors and that there wasn't anybody he would recommend more. During our many visits to Docs house I found a great fellowship with Doc and Rob that interestingly enough has now moved to Soke Rob and his senior instructors.

I witnessed Docs legacy unfold as student after student worked their way through the Hoshin System and received their Black belts under Rob's guidance. Years have passed and I am still training with the nice young man in Yorktown. Still battered and bruised on occasion but no longer in search of a

Master to help me on the path. The footprints on the path I follow look strangely like Birkenstocks."

Chris Robinson, Shihan
Hoshinbudoryu

""Rob Williams is a real wizard, you should check him out"

This was Doc Morris' endorsement of Rob and his way of telling me to go train with Rob Williams.

I first was in contact with Doc Morris after reading all of his books and seeing his e-mail address in one of them. After training in martial arts for 22 years, I was in the search for Bujinkan training. Most of Doc's energy was focused on Hoshin at the time, but he turned me on to a few "ninja" training groups a few hours from me. When I finally found someone to train with I e-mailed Doc, thanking him for helping me out.

The first time I actually met Doc was a few years later at the 2002 Bujinkan Tai Kai in St Louis. I introduced myself and told him who I was and that he had helped me out via the e-mails we had exchanged a few years earlier. Doc was a bit surprised I sought him out, I think, but was genuinely nice and compassionate. Over the next few years, I got a chance to hang out with Doc at the Texas Ninja Summits, in Wharton, Texas. We were both staying with a common friend, the host of the Summit.

Back in Virginia I had a student that had sought out a Hoshin teacher in Virginia. Since I knew Doc, I didn't really think too much of it, until that fateful day in Texas.

Doc asked me "How far are you from where they have the ships in Virginia?" I responded "You mean Norfolk?" "No, no" he replied. "Newport News?" "No, that's not it..."

"Yorktown?" I suggested, at last, struggling to match up East Coast Naval bases in the Old Dominion. He beamed a big famous Doc smile and said "Yes! That's where I was thinking of! I have a top student teaching there. Rob Williams is a real wizard, you should check him out".

I looked at my wife and realized Rob is the guy that my student had told me a bit about. As soon as we got off the plane back in Virginia, I called my student, Paul and said "Can you set up a meeting with Rob? I mean, can we go with you and train with Rob? Doc suggested we go check him out."

The next weekend, my wife Michelle and I showed up at Rob's dojo with Paul. A few other students were there as well. Rob was warm and casual and had a very friendly demeanor. Basically the next few hours turned out to be less of a "class" and more of a Hoshin "demo" with Rob using his students for the impromptu practice session. He demonstrated basic taijutsu using elemental theory. Then we started with some basic chi sensitivity drills. Even though I had seen and practiced some of this type of thing before, I was in for a big surprise. Out in broad daylight, behind the dojo where we were training and doing these drills, I looked over at Rob and saw something which I had never seen before. A white, ice blue flame was running across his shoulders and head. I looked away, rubbed my eyes discretely and looked around to see if anybody else saw what I saw. Everybody was just following along with the drill. Looking again, I saw the same thing. Now at this time I had never knowingly seen an aura, so I just kept quiet and thought I'll ask later, but there it was just as clear as day...in broad daylight!

I had a chill run up my spine, like the temp had dropped and I shivered but I couldn't stop the shivering. It was weird! Looking up, I saw Rob smiling at me and he asked "Are you OK?" "I feel like I am getting the chills."

Mind you this is July in Virginia! By the way, we are outdoors; if I hadn't mentioned it! He chuckled and walked behind me and swept the excess energy off my spine and bingo, I was fine!

Rob then went on to demonstrate some empty force by moving us as individuals and as groups. Just swaying or drawing us one direction or another. All things I had seen in a book or video, but had never felt. My wife Michelle came up and turned away from Rob about 15 feet away. As Rob drew his hands back, I watched intently to see if I saw Michelle move...

Well, the first thing I noticed was about 10 of her hairs (she had hair midway down her back) slowly raised nearly horizontal moments before she began to topple back! I kept the sight of her hair to myself. Just like the "flames" flickering around Rob's shoulders and head, I didn't want to blurt out what I was seeing. I had not really seen or knew what to look for when it came to this kind of thing. So what exactly was I seeing?

Nobody there told me I was going to see these kinds of things. Was I imagining it? I mean, I did get the chills up the spine in the bright hot Virginia sun that I could not will to stop on my own. I saw Michelle's hair lift up as if it was magnetized right before she fell over. Didn't I?

Near the end of the day Rob took us inside to show us how to view auras....Now that I knew what to look for I had to speak up.

"Rob, I saw on you...out in the direct sunlight, exactly what you are asking us to look for in the slightly shaded room, except on you I saw it crystal clear!" He laughed and said, "I was wondering if you would see that!"

Over the next year Rob and I become close friends. Doc was planning to come out to our Bujinkan dojo to do a seminar. Rob was anxious too. In fact a few weeks out, Rob emailed me and said "I have something to send you, I think Doc coming out is going to be a big deal."

Doc had on occasion referred to himself as me and Michelle's "Evil Uncle", we always got a kick out of that.

What Rob sent me really WAS something, it was a copy of an IM that Doc had with Rob just the day before. I recognized Doc's screen name immediately. Basically it made reference to Rob taking the reins of Hoshin, when Doc retired. Doc, in a phone conversation with me just a few weeks before, had said something about that too. I asked Doc, "Retiring? Well that'll be a long way off Unc'." Doc replied, "Maybe not. There are things I want to work on and Rob is my top guy. The day will come when Rob will be running the show."

That was it. We got Doc's travel plans straight to come up to do a seminar. It was supposed to be the weekend of April 1st, I had to call and reschedule because I forgot I was scheduled to participate in a 10k that weekend, so we set it up for the following weekend.

Saturday, April 1st, after the 10k, I was on a test drive with a customer, when my phone rang. It was a Hoshin/Bujinkan friend from Kentucky. He must be calling to tell me he was attending the seminar.

I answered, "Hey man! What's up?" "I just got really bad news." He said in a somber reply. I stumbled a bit, but asked "Is everything OK?"

Silence...then the words sprang from the phone, "I just got word that they found Doc Morris dead just a few minutes ago."

I pulled the truck over into an empty parking lot and threw the shifter into Park. "What?" I blurted into the phone...this had to be some sort of joke. This could not be happening! The phone crackled a bit but I clearly heard, "Do you think Rob knows?" Damn! I had to call Rob. I said my goodbyes before hanging up. I then had to explain what the call was about to my customer before dialing Rob's cell number. Rob was chipper in his greeting and I knew right away that no, he did not know. I had to break this crazy news to him. Could it be a joke? I mean it was Doc! Besides it WAS April Fool's Day!

Rob was shell shocked. He and I made a plan. He would call our friend in Kentucky to get more info and find out how he knew. Rob asked me to call Doc. Doc's cell phone went straight to voicemail. I left a message...it rambled a bit, but essentially "Doc, this is Doug. Not to sound cliché but I hope the rumors of your early demise are just that, rumors! Call me!"   Hanging up, I next dialed his home number. It seemed to ring forever, the tension was unbearable. It finally rolled to the answering machine. I basically left the same message. Rob called moments later with more details.

It seemed that indeed, Doc had in some fashion played out the ultimate April Fool's joke. Many of us thought he would be there to hold our hands along our journey.

But Doc had some place to be...

Doug Tweedy, Shidoshi
Bujinkan Shima Dojo

The Grandmaster's Story

By: Qigong Grandmaster Glenn Morris Ph.D.

The story I would like to share is about the Kundalini Awakening I experienced in the summer of 1985. I had the entire summer off from teaching and decided I was going to deeply explore some Internal Qigong practices I had known for many years. I sat on my porch and practiced intensely in Meditation running energy along my Meridians for goals I wanted to attain in the martial arts. I was utilizing the Chinese system of acupuncture points and the Hindu chakra system. I also utilized classical Taoist breathing methods and addressed the Chakras individually. I practiced everyday for about six hours due to having so much free time that summer.

After 45 days of practice I was having visions of Shiva and Kali, the legendary Hindu Gods. Later on I further experienced visual and auditory hallucinations as well as super human strength (breaking door handles from turning them too hard), reversal of lifelong arthritis, occasional bouts of telepathy and other forms of unexplainable knowing. These experiences worked up to a peak one early morning when I saw a golden brown colored viper begin to slowly uncurl from my sacrum. As if it had a mind of its own, the serpent shot its way up through my spinal column in what felt like an eruption of FIRE. It culminated with a tremendous explosion of energy in my head and I was then thoroughly 'fried'. For the next few months, when I closed my eyes there was a constant barrage of lights.

I later discovered that this was a permanent Kundalini awakening, and that is why it never went away even when I didn't practice for weeks. That energy had been released and there was no going back. I was forced to learn to live in harmony with it. After my body had fully rejuvenated and adapted to the increased voltage, I began to wonder why the 'Kundalini' experience was shrouded in myth and why I could not find a single person who had been through it themselves. I read countless books authored by people claiming to understand the Kundalini Experience and I came up empty handed. The only books I found by someone who really understood were written by Gopi Krishna and even with the help of his personal experiences, I did not fully understand what had happened to me. My only certainty was that it was a giant spiritual/biological evolutionary leap.

After spending even more time with several Kundalini Yoga experts, not only did I come up empty handed again with no answers, but I found out that this process is "supposed to" take 20-30 years of disciplined practice. Maybe that would explain why I could not find anyone who had done it. That is a long time for someone to persevere. Granted I was practicing a lot, but that did not explain why it happened within 45 days. I wanted to understand this process. I became fixated on testing and understanding. So I did what any respectable teacher would have done - I used my students as guinea pigs!!

When the same methods I used were employed by my students, they had very similar results of "Kundalini Awakening" in anywhere from 2 months to 18 months time. I watched as one after another went through the process. No one had any of the problems often written about in the 'myths' of Kundalini. We were continually amazed at the 'Universality' of the process. Later we learned that Qigong provided certain safeguards that were keeping the process safe and efficient. It was a very experimental program in the beginning. As time progressed, I refined the system further to eliminate any unnecessary practices and honed in on what was actually producing the manifestation of Kundalini. It basically came down to opening the Base Chakra (Genitals) and then working up to the higher energy centers from there. Combine the chakra work with running energy along the spine & limbs, positive mind states, employing specific breathing methods, and practicing Testicular/ Ovarian Gong Fu and you have a complete composite of what I did and what I feel is the core essence of my practice. I honestly believe these to be the most potent Qigong practices in the world.

Later I wrote 3 widely available books on the subject matter and many foreign students were emailing me from around the world reporting similar experiences from doing the practices. I decided to refine my life's work into a system we later called the "Kundalini Awakening Process". I created a highly organized program with a comprehensive workbook and home practice CD (recorded by Santiago Dobles). The workshop is taught in a weekend seminar format. The process is learned in 2 days and practiced at home along with the CD we provide you with.

The Level-1 Kundalini Awakening Process connects the sexual energy manufactured by the Genitals to the Master Glands of the Brain. If practiced for 30 minutes daily, using the Level-1 Home Practice CD, it will typically produce the Full Kundalini Awakening in around 6 to 18 months. Seasoned mediators and yoga practitioners will have much faster results sometimes within a few weeks, but really anyone can do this if they follow the instructions. The system is statistically proven to work and that's why it has a high success rate. Everything a person needs to attain the Full Kundalini Awakening is thoroughly gone over in the Level-1 training and it's all contained within the Training Manual and Home practice CD.

The Level-2 Testicular/Ovarian Gong Fu takes the Level-1 practices of opening the Root Chakra and connecting the meridians and further expounds upon them. "Male Deer" exercises for keeping sexual energy at its peak are employed in the program along with the "Female Deer" exercises, which are used to stop the menstruation process and the subsequent loss of vital energy that accompanies it. In Chinese lore the Female Deer exercises are called 'Slaying the Red Dragon' for obvious reasons. It is a very natural and powerful practice that works easily and once practice is stopped, normal menstrual periods will return immediately. It also is a great form of birth control that you can turn on and off. Both the Male and Female Deer exercises were kept highly secret by the ruling families of ancient China. The Female Deer exercises work by tricking the body into thinking its 'lactating'.

Taoist Sexual Qigong is also taught in Level -2 and can be practiced with or without a partner. These are the sexual practices of developing vital energy. Level -2 further activates the sexual energy of the Testicles/Ovaries, which has a direct impact on the Kundalini. A partner is not required, but it's more fun.

My overall theory: The Kundalini is describable and repeatable. My scholarship has taught me that Kundalini is the most powerful accumulation of latent energy potential in the human body. It has played an integral part in religious mythology, yet after watching hundreds go through the Full Process; I feel its 'Awakening' is more of a biological process than a religious one. It can be experienced by any one of significant will and intelligence to do the work.

Partial Kundalini Awakening: No Such Thing

By: Dr. Glenn J. Morris

In my humble opinion, there is no such thing as a partial Kundalini awakening. The Kundalini is a full blown experience of your spine wiring into various mystical experiences. If that's not happening, it's not Kundalini. There are experiences, such as kriyas and the development of chi, that are similar and are sometimes identified as being Kundalini experiences, but they are not. They are their own forms of phenomena and should be identified as such. The Kundalini is seldom pleasant, is almost always associated with nerve damage, periods of altered states of consciousness seeming to parallel insanity, interaction with deities, and various siddhis. At its culmination, it results in union with All. The Kundalini experience may go on for years after that. Sometimes the spiritual experiences deepen and the person becomes a true mystic, but often people just go insane.

People tell me I make it sound hazardous in all cases. It is. Hell was an important part of the journey and is for any who succeed in enduring the Kundalini. Most feel that the heart will guide, but it doesn't seem to work that way in the majority of cases. Partial experiences may be feeling energy move through the body, particularly up and down the spine, occasional altered states that quickly fade, some siddhis, skill in healing, increased energy, seeing auras, or mood and appetite alterations. People often treat this as if it was a Kundalini awakening, but in my opinion that's just wishful thinking. It's chi development and if people do not follow a schedule of chi kung, they'll eventually get into trouble with it, usually with kidney or liver failure. Oftentimes, these partial Kundalini effects are brought on by mixing drug use with meditation or intense Chi Kung training as used in the martial arts. The effects fade away if you quit meditating or breathing in a Chi Kung manner or, in the case of drug use, when the effects wear off. It's safer to take the slower path of meditation and following the breath. As far as achieving enlightenment, the Kundalini is the rocket path, but cannot be followed. It's its own phenomenon. Until it happens, it's good to do Zen meditation, chi kung, or follow a bhakti tradition in preparing the body and mind.

Dr. Glenn J. Morris experienced a full Kundalini awakening starting in 1985. This article originally appeared as a letter on a Kundalini mail list on February 12, 2000.

Bibliography

These are books I read that helped me in understanding a particular area of study. They are grouped by subject and are the best opinions I could find regarding each topic. I recommend reading them as though you are having a conversation with the author. No one knows everything. If you like something, try it out. If it doesn't work after real effort has been given, try something else. Reading is an important part of Hoshin training. You should also read all of the books in the bibliographies of Dr. Morris' books. I include his works here, as well as the books I have enjoyed the most.

Martial Arts

Glenn J. Morris Path Notes of an American Ninja Master Berkley, California: North Atlantic Books, 1993

Glenn J. Morris Shadow Strategies of an American Ninja Master Berkley, California: Frog Ltd, 1996

Glenn J. Morris Martial Arts Madness: A User's Guide to the Esoteric Martial Arts

Glenn J. Morris Quantum Crawfish Bisque for the Clueless Soul: How Choice Works to Create Success or Despair Available as an e-book through Umaatantra.com 2006

Masaaki Hatsumi Essence of Ninjutsu: The Nine Traditions Chicago, Illinois: Contemporary Books, Inc. 1988

Masaaki Hatsumi Ninpo: Wisdom for Life Yonkers, New York: Mushashin Press 1998

Masaaki Hatsumi & Benjamin Cole Understand? Good. Play! Words of Consequence Bushin Books 2001

Masaaki Hatsumi Unarmed Fighting Techniques of the Samurai Tokyo, Japan: Kodansha International Ltd. 2008

Vladimir Vasiliev The Russian System Guidebook: Inside Secrets of Soviet Special Forces Training Visalia, California: Optimum Training Systems 1997

Wally Jay Small Circle Jujutsu Santa Clarita, California: Ohara Publications Inc. 1989

William Scott Wilson The Lone Samurai: The Life of Miyamoto Musashi Tokyo, Japan: Kodansha International Ltd. 2004

Stephen K. Hayes Enlightened Self-Protection; The Kasumi-An Ninja Arts Tradition Germantown, Ohio: Nine Gates Press 1992

Steven K Hayes Ninja Realms of Power: Spiritual Roots and Traditions of the Shadow Warrior Chicago, Illinois: Contemporary Books Inc. 1986

Paul Dong and Thomas Raffill Empty Force: The Ultimate Martial Art Boston, Massachusetts: Element Books Inc. 1996

Healing

Gary A. Thibodeau Structure and Function of the Body St. Louis, Missouri: Mosby-Year Book, Inc. 1997

Mark F. Beck Milady's Theory and practice of Therapeutic Massage Albany, New York: Milady Publishing, 1999.

Alice Burmeister w/ Tom Monte The Touch of Healing New York, New York: Bantam Books 1997.

Frances M. Tappan Healing Massage Techniques: Holistic, Classic and Emerging Methods Norwalk, Connecticut: Appleton & Lange 1988

Randolph Stone Polarity Therapy: The Complete Collected Works Vol. 1 & 2 Summertown, Tennessee: CRCS Wellness Books 1954-1957

Marsha Burack Reiki- Healing Yourself and Others Encinitas, California: Reiki Healing Institute 1995

Ilana Rubenfeld The Listening Hand: Self Healing Through The Rubenfeld Synergy Method of Touch and Talk New York, New York: Bantam Books 2000

Deepak Chopra Quantum Healing: Exploring the Frontiers of Mind/ Body Medicine New York, New York: Bantam Books 1989

Toyoko Matsuzari The Healing Power of Hado Hillsboro, Oregon: Beyond Words Publishing, Inc. 2005

Moshe Feldenkrais Awareness Through Movement New York, New York: HarperCollins Publishers 1990

Kundalini Awakening

Ajit Mookerjee Kundalini, The Arousal of the Inner Energy
Rochester, Vermont: Destiny Books 1982

John White Kundalini, Evolution and Enlightenment Garden
City, New York: Anchor Books 1979

Gopi Krishna Kundalini: The Evolutionary Energy in Man
Boston, Massachusetts: Shambhala Publications, Inc. 1997

Stuart Sovatsky Eros, Consciousness, and Kundalini Rochester,
New York: Park Street Press 1999

Ravindra Kumar Kundalini for Beginners St. Paul, Minnesota:
Llewellyn Publications 2000

Other Books offered by the Hoshinbudoryu

These books can be purchased from our website
www.hoshin.us

John Porter & Rob Williams The Psions' Guide Lulu
Publishing 2007

John Porter Hoshin Games Lulu Publishing 2007

Rob Williams Hoshin Healing Manual originally released
spring of 2003

Index

The following emails and quotes are included at the request of my students and affiliates. A few emails are presented in their entirety with Dr. Glenn Morris' words in **bold**. They reinforce the events I describe in the previous chapters. The complete texts of some emails have been included so that nothing is taken out of context. Headers endorsing a particular email server have been removed as well as email addresses. These are Doc's words. They are in no way meant to be an accusation of anything or anyone. Pay attention to the dates on them. The words are from the horse's mouth. I stand behind the validity of these quotes. I have many more but some portions of them are too personal to share.

Email from Glenn Morris
to Gord Hessie and Rob Williams

Re: Good Morning

Wednesday, February 2, 2005 8:11 PM
From: "Glenn Morris" <spider1@structurex.net>
To: "Gord Hessie", "Rob Williams"

Try ninpo777@yahoo.com for Rob.
----- Original Message -----
From: Gord Hessie
To: Glenn Morris
Sent: Wednesday, February 02, 2005 3:03 PM
Subject: Re: Good Morning

How can I get a hold of Rob? Where does he live?

Virginia

I think it is probably a good idea to get that piece of the puzzle from him. He is better at it than I am. I consider him my successor.

I want this dojo here to be a pure Hoshin club. Of course I will use your materials. I want this to be huge and successful. I also need to get up to speed on the healing portion.

You are a great technician. Hoshin has a lot of woo woo factor. Meditation, chi kung, sensing, telempathy, massage, nontouch healing.

To have genuine credibility, this dojo should not have primary instructors at the shodan level.

Sandan in ninjutsu is pretty high. JUst hang the weapons on the wall. Get with ian and rob for syllabi etc. We'll get you to nidan and sandan quick enough. Just wear a black belt and growl occasionally. We don't want to geta wussy rep.like the new ninja.

I need to get to work. Any help from you would be greatly appreciated.

Looking forward to your input,
Gord

Glenn Morris to Rob Williams
2 ½ months prior to his passing

Re: Fwd: [Fwd: Pending activity for hoshinchat group will soon expire]

Monday, January 16, 2006 10:49 PM
From: "glenn m" <spidersoke@yahoo.com>
To: "Rob Williams" <ninpo777@yahoo.com>

Comments below:

--- Rob Williams <ninpo777@yahoo.com> wrote:
 sign in to yahoo under spidersoke. then go to the main yahoo page and click on groups. search for hoshin chat, then click on join this group. there is no moderators... just a public forum. i searched the archives and didn't see any recent posts. should put you back in the mix.

Oh well. Don't understand why it requests moderation from time to time. Then it won't recognize me.

Kai Zen in Alaska. How do you think attendance would be?

At least as good as Italy. Lots of folks on the west coast that would enjoy an authentic training with Yupik eskimos. I think I'll set it out about a year so they can save their shekels up. Noonkesser likes orienteering too. He and Porter can run a course through some serious wilderness.

Do you think we would have a good turn out? Folks were pissed about the Kai zen in Italy. Thats why we did NOT the Kai Zen.

People better get used to the idea that I'm international
and hoshin has members around the world. Wanna go to
England? When you are running this show, do you think you can
bring it all to Richmond. In Italy we had people from Germany,
Nederlands, France, Sweden, Belgium, and England. We are
more than nationwide.

food for thought.

It made me question why I bother keeping some people around.
I've done a lot more for most of these guys than they have done
for me. They don't want me chewing on those thoughts. Glenn

Glenn Morris to Doug Tweedy

Re: Potential dates for Richmond seminar

Tuesday, November 29, 2005 4:25 PM
From: "glenn m" <spidersoke@yahoo.com>
To: Wdtweedy@aol.com, "Rob Williams"
<hoshinbudo@yahoo.com>, "Glenn Morris"
<spider1@structurex.net>
Lets go for for Mar 25/26. Talk to Rob.

I charge for the plane ticket, expenses, training fees of $750.00 a
day. Since I like to get to know people you can save a lot of
money by putting me up. I usually like that better than a hotel.

I'll teach, given our conversation: Martial meditation techniques
for internal and external power: Secret smile and fear reduction.
(Actually battle tested by Louisiana National Guard in
Baghdad.)

Aura seeing and feeling for healing and martial applications.

Basic Dim Mak, Energy points that enhance your techniques and weaken your opponent.

Meridian massage for integrating energy movement.

The Hoshin Syllabus and why you should learn a chakra based system of combative martial arts. Applying science to your art through function, form, and energetics. We'll turn you guys into the local hoshin gurus. Rob can teach whatever he thinks is his best seminar material that won't make me look too bad and decrepit. Should I bring swords? No we'll keep this yogaish first time out of the box. Glenn
--- Wdtweedy@aol.com wrote:

Dr. Morris,
Thanks so much for taking my call the other night, I really enjoyed chatting with you. It looks like we are available any weekend in March, right now. Just let me know what dates are best for you. Also if you could pass on information regarding the cost and requirements (travel, lodging, seminar fees, etc.) and we can get the ball rolling, on our end. I look forward to hearing from you!

Doug Tweedy

Quotes & E-mails from Doc

Jan 11 2006. Glenn talking to Rob regarding the seminar they were supposed to teach in March 06, later Glenn pushed the date back to April 1st, then April 15th. Rob held the seminar in Glenn's honor.

March 18th and 19th are great. Enjoyed talking to you too. Time to get our marketing together. Rewrite the websites. I'm thinking of you and Mark and Tina as the models of what hoshin is going to be as an organization.

We'll give them Basics of meditation for martial arts

Secret Smile and orbit

Seeing and Feeling the Aura

Hoshin balance points, body movement, and self-protection.

Death Touch (Three points each) favorites

Howzdat?

Feb 7th 2006. Glenn Morris.

Ah well. I'm doing a seminar in Virginia in April. Rob will fill you in. He likes the rooskis too. I'm working for the VOA and giving chi rubs to cops and firemen. Great fun. We've integrated some of the russian stuff ino Hoshin at the BB level. Most of the ninpo guys are too impressed with their kamae to get the russian flow. Glenn

Jan 18th, 2006 Glenn Morris

Always interesting, but none of us are blemish free. I'm usually willing to play along but I don't like to be exploited for my effort. That seems to be my karma.

November 12th, 2004. Rob and Glenn discussing the Hoshinroshiryu Belt videos and the syllabus Rob was putting together for Glenn.

I want YOU to make dvds of the first and second star of each belt and then they have to get with a teacher for the third. We'll give them the first two belts as distant learning but they have to link up with someone for the rest. Go for it. EXPLAIN ALL THE SNEAKY LEVERAGE AND DAMAGE AS YOU GO. Have the yoga packages in the works now. Great stuff. Glenn

--- Rob Williams wrote:

Doc, rough with out the physiology and psychology page. These are the outlines I made for my class. All of it is core Hoshin. I have been working on easy ways to defeat ninpo kihon. I can destroy all the kamae and sword and stick work too. It is soooo Hoshin; smooth and nasty. The counters I have seen ninja do are much more athletic. You are going to love it. Wait till you see my Shodan manual.

Rob Williams
Hoshin Budo Association

Rob and Glenn discussing an incident in class

Good story. That will happen from time to time. Nice you gave him the near death experience. It seems to hurry their conversion. They never seem to realize we are offering our bodies ... As for the energy. You are definitely a vampire. If you are tired you keep running the orbit and burn it up. Double pun there. Returning it to earth is a good a way to dump excess as any if you

don't want to store it in the gut. You seem to have the right instincts. Glenn

I watched Ruling Class the other night. What a great movie. I'll definitely show it in 205. Glenn

Glenn J. Morris, Ph.D., Sc. D.
Prof. of Org. Comm.
Mc Neese State University
Speech & Theatre

www.hoshinjutsu.org
----- Original Message -----
From: Rob Williams
To: Glenn J. Morris
Sent: Monday, March 19, 2001 1:02 PM
Subject: another "Let's test the teacher" incident/question

Soke, I had a student decide to test me during chain technique training. We use plastic chain and the ends are cloth tape. I was showing the techniques, basic swings and blocks...etc I had a real kusari that I was letting them try out to really feel the weight. One of the students comes up behind me and grabs me in the over the arms from behind bear hug. He is your size and picked me up easily, squeezing with all his might. I made myself heavy and as his strength was going he tried to throw me sideways. I shifted my weight back toward him and ended up on my feet standing, facing him, shoulder to shoulder. He still had a hold of me. I did a shark bite to his inner thigh...he still was trying to put up a fight. He said to me " I like to wrestle, It's fun!" as he again trys to throw me over. I grabbed the lapel w/ the right hand, his groin with my left and dumped him over! He tried to roll over be he didn't realize I had his scrotum pinched. I held him there, upside down, hanging from my hand as I asked in a calm tone," Are we through playing?" He very quickly said YES!!

The rest of my class just kind of looked at him like "What the fuck are you thinking, Chris?"

 I proceeded to calmly show escapes from reverse bear hugs on the same guy. His bear hug from then on was very light. At the end of class I showed healing stuff with Chris as the patient.   My question is when situations like that arise, I feel myself draining energy off of them. It goes around the orbit and then I send to my feet and out. I shake it off my hands too. They get to their normal ice cold. What should I be doing with this energy? I always think to dump it back to mother earth but is this what I should be doing? Thank you for you guidance, Rob W

Excerpts from *Quantum Crawfish Bisque for the Clueless Soul: How Choice Helps Create Success or Despair* Glenn J. Morris 2006

"Rob Williams has systemized the healing side of Hoshin into a distance learning system with a certification program in budo massage."

"Healing of subtle injuries was probably one of the early forms of mental therapy and works pretty well for more mundane injuries as Rob Williams, who is nationally certified in massage therapy and heads up our budo massage therapy can verify."

www.ingramcontent.com/pod-product-compliance
Lightning Source LLC
Chambersburg PA
CBHW031042110426
42740CB00046B/525